I0453198

THE
ATLANTEAN
CODE:
HEALING WITH THE ENERGIES
OF ATLANTIS

ISABELLE ST GERMAIN
The cover image was created by Dominique Huser

Copyright © Year 2025

All Rights Reserved by **Isabelle St Germain.**

No part of this publication may be reproduced in any form, or by any means, electronic or mechanical, including photocopying, recording, or any information browsing, storage, or retrieval system, without permission in writing from Isabelle St Germain.

First Edition — 2025

ISBN
Hardcover: 979-8-90190-030-7
Paperback: 979-8-90190-029-1

"I invite you to discover my world and feel free to contact me!"
Website: https://isabellestgermain.com
Email: isabellestgermain2022@gmail.com
Youtube: Isabelle St Germain
Facebook: Isabelle St-Germain

THE ATLANTEAN CODE

HEALING WITH THE ENERGIES OF ATLANTIS

ISABELLE ST GERMAIN

Table of Contents

Note to the Reader

It is important to understand that I never encourage anyone to stop taking medication, allopathic treatments or forgo psychological support without their doctor's approval and guidance.

The purpose of this book is to help you understand the functioning of your holistic body. I will teach you how to harness your creative power and force to regain better overall health and achieve optimal quality of life.

I also want to share the knowledge and sacred energetic tools that you can use to neutralize and release disqualified energies.

This book is by no means intended to replace or serve as a substitute for any form of medical, psychological, or psychotherapeutic consultation.

Throughout this book, I've used words such as God, Initial Sacred, Initial Sacred-Breast and Sacred Radiance. It is important to understand the energetic vibrations these words carry if you wish to achieve better results.

However, I want you to keep in mind that these words are not associated with any specific religion. Also, to make the reading feel lighter, I've used the masculine form of writing and included the feminine voice too, where the context required it.

*To **Annie Poirier**, whose insight and guidance helped bring clarity and structure to these pages.*

My heartfelt thanks also go to everyone who contributed their time and expertise in editing and formatting this work.

Preamble

Life has always been seen as a great mystery. And yet, if you only knew how much this powerful vibration animating everything that exists is overflowing with extraordinary knowledge—accessible to each and every one of us—you would be amazed!

The purpose of this book is precisely to share with you my great and powerful discoveries of the past 20 years, and more specifically, the treasures of Atlantean knowledge and its sacred energetic tools. I sincerely wish to help you understand and integrate that transformation is simple and easy to achieve when you learn to apply certain basic principles.

What has been revealed to me through my extensive research and ongoing mystical experiences goes far beyond human understanding. Thanks to these fascinating journeys through time, across different dimensions, spaces, and vibrational planes, I have been able to recover the knowledge of my soul. I certainly do not claim to have discovered everything! I still continue to explore and discover, with great joy and gratitude, new realms overflowing with precious and sacred information—some of which have had a very positive impact, and at times a less positive one, on my life and my physical, emotional, psychic, and psychological well-being. I see the same dazzling results every day in both my students and my clients.

It was by integrating the power of the science of the word at an unexpected level that everything began to make sense to me. When I understood that everything could be transformed instantly by learning to reactivate—differently and very effectively—the science behind the well-known saying: "Ask and you shall receive," the magic of life began to work its miracles within me and all around me!

You will soon realize that even though the physical body is designed in a complex way, it is truly possible for you to experience both small and very large transformations on every level, including your physical health. Additionally, understand that age does not impact the results you want to achieve. The process is the same for everyone.

I can already hear you questioning: "Is it truly possible that we have the ability to act and intervene in our physical, emotional, psychic, psychological health—and even that of others—so easily?"

In response to all these questions, I will share my story with you. I will explain what has shaped me into who I am today. Know that no matter who you are, you will find answers to your questions, along with practical, easy exercises you can integrate into your daily life. You will also joyfully discover that you are completely normal, for everything coexists and everything is absolutely possible. It is up to each individual to reactivate the science of the word in order to gain remarkable results.

To fully benefit from your reading, I strongly suggest avoiding interpretation through the lens of a controlling, directive mind. Through these pages, you will embark on a journey with your creative power. I invite you to settle comfortably into the sacred space of your heart, in your own unique way, and to set the intention to receive this knowledge at a deep cellular level, and throughout your holistic being. By doing so, you will incorporate all the teachings I am about to share with you quickly and naturally.

Furthermore, I hope this book will provide a joyful, powerful, and engaging experience for you, my dear readers. I'm excited to share that you'll have real-time access to various exercises, enabling you to assimilate the new concepts you'll learn immediately. You'll always have the choice to either continue your captivating reading or jump to the suggested exploratory exercise, depending on your inspiration in the moment.

Each time you see this symbol ♥, you can go directly to the suggested page and practice to deepen your new learning in a tangible way.

I firmly believe that by taking the time to put this newly acquired knowledge into practice that it truly becomes anchored in our holistic being, our cells and our daily lives. Therefore, I invite you to be always guided by the Sacred Radiance of your heart, to know what you need, here and now. Everything is always right and perfect and arrives at the right time in our evolutionary journey.

Achieving lasting results requires strong determination, unwavering willpower, and Faith in oneself. Just speaking of Faith in oneself will likely surprise many of you, as it has been misused by religion, medicine and major professions. That is not the truth of it.

Faith is a divine vibrational and sonic frequency that should resonate strongly within you at all times. It holds a powerful inner force that aligns you with the truth of your heart. Once it is activated and intensified, everything becomes clear in terms of your thoughts and what you need to do or accomplish.

Are you ready for the Adventure? Let's go!!

Introduction

Every person who incarnates on Earth has a life mission to fulfill. To help you better grasp this important concept, I will share my thoughts with you throughout these pages. I will offer you precious teachings that will support your own mission and personal evolution. I humbly admit that I would have greatly appreciated knowing this information from a very young age. It would have helped me better understand why I had to go through so many truly difficult experiences throughout my life.

I assure you that after these rather destabilizing events, I had to learn to develop faith and absolute trust in who I am, in my creative power of love, and in everything that cannot be perceived with our earthly eyes. Before delving deeper into my story, I would like to introduce you to some important concepts regarding life's purpose.

Love of Self and Others

Know that the very first thing all humans have come to accomplish on this Earth is to relearn how to love themselves, to fully accept themselves, and to live their lives out of love for themselves. Why? Because in the soul's past incarnations, this power of love was almost exclusively directed toward others, animals, and objects.

But what exactly is love?

It is essential to distinguish between truly loving oneself and others, and the illusion of love driven by fear and unhealed soul wounds.

Even today, society views self-love as a form of selfishness. This false belief often hinders the divine growth of many individuals who, wanting to be seen as a "good, loving person," choose to forget themselves completely in order to help others endlessly.

This behavior is not at all aligned with the truth of your mission on Earth. You will notice that when you choose to follow this path of illusory love, your body will gladly alert you. It will send you warning signals of varying intensity based on your actions, to help you become aware that it's more than time to truly relearn how to love yourself.

For example, you may increasingly feel empty inside, as if your life has lost its meaning. You may also feel physically and emotionally drained when you make choices that go against your true nature.

Does this resonate with you?

Let me reassure you: reconnecting with self-love absolutely does not mean you have to stop helping others! It means taking time to recharge, to pause and to make conscious choices filled with love for yourself. This is about learning to offer yourself the best in everything so you can give back the best version of who you are.

Thus, you'll understand that it is essential for each of us to allow ourselves to reactivate this great sacred Radiance of love toward ourselves on every level.

It is by consciously choosing to live from the truth of your heart that you will discover the fast track to all the knowledge your soul carries. This key that you hold is extremely precious, because the more you connect to the truth of your heart—this powerful frequency of infinite love—the more amazed you'll be to discover the universe of infinite possibilities available to you!

Let's talk a bit more in detail about what true love is. It feels like a powerful surge from the heart that empowers us to embrace ourselves and others as we are, with kindness, without judgment, without criticism or expectation. That feeling of being free from all forms of possessiveness, guilt, ownership, self-destruction, self-sabotage and attachment allows us to feel completely free, with our heart wide open to all that is.

Embodying true love connects us to all our inner riches, such as the freedom to be, the joy of existing, peace, serenity, well-being, happiness, self-confidence and the recognition of our priceless value—faith, abundance, and self-respect, among others. Remember, love is not an emotion but a state of the soul.

True love also means embodying with certainty the awareness that, after ourselves, all the beings who orbit within our universe are the most important people in our lives. Every moment we choose to spend with those around us is a divine appointment that was arranged long before we incarnated on Earth. The celestial plan is grand!

Truly loving may seem very easy at first glance, and yet, a great number of people self-sabotage because they believe they do not deserve love and are therefore unworthy of it. The environment and upbringing you experienced during your younger years most often determine your ability to receive and give love.

To help you better understand this concept, I invite you to visualize the following two scenarios:

Imagine a child who grew up in an environment where every day, his parents repeatedly told him that he was worthless, simply because his school grades consistently fell below average. This chipped away at his self-worth, reinforcing this belief that he could never be good enough.

Now imagine this same child who, throughout his life, has heard that he will never accomplish anything good, that his dreams are out of reach, all because he lacks intelligence. Can you feel the weight of those words pressing down on his spirit?

The consequences of these devastating words on the lives of these developing young individuals are immense. At that age, the brain does not possess the discernment capacity of an adult brain. These words, therefore, have a direct impact on their confidence, self-esteem, and faith in themselves. Many mental illnesses actually stem from this. Often, these unhealthy behaviors and words from parents reflect their own difficult yet unconscious childhood patterns.

But how can we break free from that?

The journey of accepting and acknowledging what has been experienced, said, or thought is a magical key that will allow you to regain inner peace quickly.

Instead of deeply repressing your suffering, you choose to simply acknowledge that it happened. This does not mean that you agree with what was done, said, or thought. It means that, out of love for yourself, you are making the conscious choice to cultivate peace within your entire being.

Here's a clue to know whether you've truly freed yourself:

Connect at the level of your heart and bring your awareness to the experience you wish to transform. If you feel a surge of love when thinking about it, that means you've succeeded. If you feel tightness, it would be helpful to repeat the exercise.

It is completely natural for it to take several attempts before achieving full release.

I'm curious—are you aware of having experienced situations, words, gestures, or events from your childhood that were difficult and still hinder your life energy today?

I invite you to take a moment to close your eyes, to consult with yourself and to ask your soul to bring back to your memory anything that has not yet been forgiven, accepted, or acknowledged.

I recommend writing this precious information in a notebook. This way, you will have concrete examples to work with during the next chapters.

I sincerely thank you for the beautiful steps you are choosing to take here and now out of love for yourself.

If you would like to experience this new concept, go directly to page 135, exercise #1.

Enjoy the discovery! The Basic Procedure

Being Fully Responsible for Your Life

Did you know that everything you are experiencing right now in your life, as well as everything you have experienced in the past, was drawn to you by each of your thoughts, words, or actions? This is what we call the law of cause and effect, linked to the science of your word. The more you are able to accept and recognize full responsibility for your immense creative power, the more you will regain access to your great ability to create your dream life with ease.

To begin noticing real changes in your daily life, you'll need to develop a strong presence within yourself by choosing your words wisely, the thoughts you nurture and the actions you take. Everything you emit will always return to you.

At the same time, I invite you to cultivate a space of kindness toward yourself and use these teachings to get to know yourself better. Learn to develop the new ability to observe yourself consciously, at every moment. You'll quickly realize how exciting it is to reclaim your personal power and manifest joyfully and effortlessly everything you wish to see realized in your life.

Loving oneself is both an art and a treasure, and very few people succeed easily or quickly.

Who can say that their word is impeccable, that their thoughts are always positive? At the same time, I invite you to truly have fun—lightheartedly—witnessing all the new miracles that each small and big change will bring into your life! Let me tell you: divine justice is completely neutral. Now that you know this great secret, it's your move!

Now I'd like to highlight the impact of your words and thoughts. You are creators, so it's important to understand that simply stopping your conversations won't resolve your little problems. During my own learning process, that was the first thing I considered: if I stopped speaking, there would be no more unpleasant experiences.

What I hadn't realized then was that my thoughts were just as powerful as my words. It's also important to remember that you can manifest beautiful and magnificent things as well—it's not all necessarily negative.

Also, very often, when someone has an extraordinary experience, the first thing they say is, "It's thanks to him or her that this happened to me." However, when something unpleasant happens, they immediately say, "Of course—it only ever happens to me!"

When the experience is beautiful, you should feel proud and take all the credit. You made it happen in your life, not someone else.

One night, while working on two workshop booklets, it was around 1 a.m. and I hadn't finished. I decided it was time to sleep, but Master Saint-Germain said, "We're not done yet!"

I stopped and replied, "I know, but I'll finish tomorrow." He insisted that I complete the entire booklet.

Following that experience, I started saying that the beings of light were pushing me in the ass so I would write faster. I said it over and over again, and I ended up with a hemorrhoid flare-up that lasted five weeks. On top of that, I kept saying that once it was over, I'd have a flaming-hot ass... Well, let me tell you, it kept burning more and more, and I didn't know how to sit anymore. I can confirm that it is *not* the beings of light who are pushing us in the ass!

Another time, it was about -40 degrees Celsius outside, and I needed to leave my apartment on the second floor. I had a large staircase to descend and a heavy wooden door that kept out the winter cold. I couldn't pull the door shut behind me. After several attempts, the only way I could shut it was with a big shove, creating a loud noise that echoed throughout the neighborhood.

After slamming it a few more times, my landlord, who lived just below me, rang my doorbell. I asked him to close the door because I was the one paying for the electricity. He yelled at me for ten minutes, accusing me of breaking the door and saying I was no longer welcome and that my lease wouldn't be renewed.

He left, and I closed the door the only way I could once more. Back upstairs, my partner at the time looked at me and said, "Do you realize this is your fault?" I gave him a deadly glare—I expected compassion and hoped he'd take my side. I'll spare you the details of what I said.

But his words echoed in my mind that night. Believe it or not, when I first visited that apartment—my first home in Montreal—I didn't feel safe. I had prioritized finding my daughter's school before securing the apartment. When the landlord called the next day to say I was accepted, I returned to sign the lease and was surprised to see a "For Sale" sign in front of the house.

When I signed, I told him he wouldn't sell the house, because I didn't plan on moving right away. That conversation resurfaced in my memory. The next morning, I went to tell him I would leave peacefully if I was no longer welcome. We talked for 10 to 15 minutes, and when I returned home, the same door, unrepaired, closed naturally as if it had never been broken.

All this to say: we do *not* have the right to block someone's desires or projects. This happened nearly 25 years ago. And even though I've known since I was a teenager that my words are powerful, I hadn't yet realized the extent to which I could manifest such experiences.

I experienced several returns of my words while living there. For example, when I came home from work after 6 p.m., I often had to park two streets away because I didn't have a private parking space. I began to feel it was embarrassing to own a car in Montreal. Naturally, two months later, when I went to retrieve my car for work, I found that it had been stolen overnight.

At that time, I worked at a finance company, and every morning the mailman delivered gray envelopes filled with client payments. I asked him if he could deliver a huge bouquet of flowers instead, just for fun, with no expectations. I made this request for two weeks. My boss told me I needed to stop dreaming in Technicolor.

One day, I returned from lunch and a colleague said, "You arrived just in time—someone's here for you." I walked forward and all I could see was an enormous bouquet of flowers hiding the person's face. They handed me the flowers and a card that read: "With no expectations, just for the joy of giving them to you!"

You can imagine the look my boss gave me…

You see, it's entirely possible to manifest exactly what you desire. I'm someone who talks a lot—it helps in my work. However, what's less enjoyable is that I often have to use words with less positive connotations to help my clients understand the root of their suffering. All those words come out of *my* mouth—and if I don't neutralize their impact, the return happens quickly.

When I asked my guides why, they kindly explained that I possess the knowledge and energetic tools to clear those effects. That it's my responsibility to use them—nothing more.

When I say, we cling to many beliefs—I'm not exempt, far from it. Everything comes back to me at lightning speed. Just because I help people transform their lives doesn't mean I can say whatever I want without consequences.

We speak thousands of words every day. Do you think that everything you say serves your highest good?

The best way to know what you'll experience in the coming days, weeks, and months is simple—and you don't need a crystal ball.

Next time you're having dinner with friends or family, turn on your phone's recording function and forget about it. The next day, listen to everything you said. Be warned: you probably won't enjoy hearing those emotionally charged words.

Write down the key takeaways from the recording and let time reveal to you that you are a powerful creator. From experience, I know that—

even after many transformations—old habits often return quickly in family settings. Old expressions, trying to top each other's stories... You name it. It's the most insightful experience and also the hardest to undo.

I'll share the steps to learn how to neutralize the impact of your words or thoughts. Understand this, with perseverance, you can achieve your goals. There's no fatality—remember, we always get a second chance.

Many people have told me, "You know, Isabelle, if I use my second chance and mess up again, that's it—it's over, and I'll just have to wait for the consequences."

That's when I explain that having a second chance means you can repeat the process as many times as necessary to neutralize the destructive impact on your life, body, past, present, and future. Everything happens in the present moment.

Conduct the experiment and you'll quickly realize how beautifully life is designed. It all depends on *you* and how much you want to see what is dear to your heart come true.

Sometimes, I wonder if it's possible to have a little bell ring in my ears every time a thought or word is out of alignment with what life most wants to give me. Honestly, I know it's possible, but I also feel it would ring *very* often! Ha ha ha!

Learning to laugh at your own results isn't always easy, but instead of feeling guilty, if you just laughed out loud, it wouldn't take hours or days to move on to something better for yourself.

Once you understand, accept, and recognize that the power of your creative ability is infinite, you'll begin to use your words and thoughts to serve you. I'm convinced of it.

A few years ago, as I discovered that I could manifest emotional healing spheres, which seemed to bring faster results—I hadn't yet realized I was always asking for healing on an *emotional* level, not a *physical* one.

I manifested many spheres, each and very powerful. And yes, big transformations occurred for those who experienced them. But nothing remained in the physical body. I didn't understand why—until recently.

I don't remember what I was doing, but suddenly, it felt like the revelation of the century. The disappointment was immense. I couldn't believe I had never realized what I was asking for. Every time I used a sphere, I named it. But clearly, I wasn't ready to hear it.

Once I accepted this insight, I sat down and called upon the Specialists of Atlantis. I chose to manifest a healing sphere for the physical body, taking my time to clearly specify everything I wanted it to include.

When I experienced it, I felt many releases in my physical body, especially in my respiratory system, which is the most active part of my body since it's directly connected to my words and thoughts.

I was amazed. You need to know—I rarely felt physical sensations from using energetic tools. I often said I saw nothing, felt nothing, and heard nothing—since I possess *claircognizance*.

It was everyday life that showed me the results of using energetic tools. You can imagine how significant this realization was, just like when I discovered emotional healing spheres.

I had many releases, acceptances, and recognitions to process in order to reset everything I had energetically fed to zero point. I'm so grateful to have these precious tools. Without them, it would have taken me years to release all of it.

You are the most important person in your life. You must give to yourself before giving to others. I also advise you never to give a gift you wouldn't dream of receiving.

First, you may not truly please the person who receives it. Second, you might feel disheartened by their reaction when they unwrap it.

I bring this up because how many times have you felt an emptiness inside?

How many times have you believed that finding a romantic partner would fill that void?

If you think about it, at first, you're on cloud nine, but very soon, that empty space comes right back. Some people eat to fill that void. Others take up extreme sports.

In the end, what you need to know is that *you are empty of yourself.*

If you'd like to explore this new concept, go immediately to page 137, exercise #2.

Enjoy the discovery! Releasing the Impact of My Words and Thoughts

Beliefs and Expressions to Transform

This brings me to talk to you about the many beliefs that have been residing within you since childhood, often without your even realizing it. Let's start with everything related to money. What did you hear about it when you were little? That you have to work hard to succeed? That you must save money for tough times? That to become someone important, you need to have a lot of money? That money is dirty and rich people have no heart?

Just reading those questions—do any of them still ring true for you today?

Money is simply an energy, like any other. Do you associate your value with the amount in your bank account?

Sincerely, I hope you understand by now that there will never be enough money on Earth to buy you. Let me say it again—you are priceless.

How many times did your parents or relatives tell you that certain things shouldn't be said or done? If you think about it, many topics were taboo and often rooted in religious teachings. Today, those same subjects frequently become a source of emotional repression because you bought into the belief that they were off-limits.

The question is: *Are you still that little child who has to do and say only what their parents approve of, or do you now dare to express and assert yourself?*

Too often, the belief that you must lower your eyes before authority or someone of higher social status still lingers from childhood. By lowering your eyes, you're agreeing that the person in front of you is more important and more valuable than you are.

I suggest you revisit this belief, because the more you look people in the eye, the more you'll realize that they are just human beings like you who have simply made different choices.

At first, it won't be easy. Remember: we tend to be comfortable in our old shoes. But your self-esteem and confidence will grow day by day.

How many times were you told not to bother others, that you were capable of handling things on your own?

If you heard these words repeatedly, it may now be difficult to reach out to someone for a little help. But know this—a simple piece of advice can often change everything.

Dare to call the person who comes to mind—your intuition is always right.

What about everything you've absorbed regarding the fear of disappointing your parents?

I invite you to create a list of everything you do out of obligation rather than joy, simply because your parents repeated: *"Whatever you do, don't disappoint us!"*

Do you still feel that fear surface whenever you dare to take a path different from theirs?

If you followed your own direction while still feeding the fear of disappointing them, you likely didn't succeed fully and gave them another reason to say, *"We warned you not to do this or that!"*

It is so important to trust yourself.

If an idea contrary to your parents is looping in your thoughts, it's undoubtedly pointing you toward what you're meant to do.

But you must vibrate with trust and faith throughout the journey and the results will be phenomenal.

Did you know that a woman whose mother and grandmother suffered from the same illness at roughly the same age will likely fear developing that illness herself as she nears that age?

Remember, our words and thoughts are incredibly creative. As soon as the fear or anticipation of developing the same illness arises, you can be sure it will manifest.

So, if your family constantly repeats things like, *"Do you realize you're getting close to the age when mom and grandma..."*

I ask you to put a stop to such conversations and tell them:

"I am not my mother or my grandmother, and I'm putting an end to these repetitive patterns of illness passed down from generation to generation. I am healthy and happy to be so."

Once again, let go and stop feeding that belief.

Here are some expressions to replace:

- "That really blows me away!"
- *Likely result:* Weight gain and bloating.
- → Replace with: "That makes me a billionaire."
- "It's doing my head in!"
- *Likely result:* Tension and headaches.
- → Replace with: "That makes me a billionaire."
- "I can't digest that person!"
- *Likely result:* Digestive issues.
- → Replace with: "My relationship with this person is really not easy."
- "That'll cost an arm and a leg."
- *Likely result:* Arm pain.
- → Replace with: "That's going to be expensive."
- "It's hard not to say this or that."
- *Likely result:* Difficulty in life.
- → Replace with: "It's really not easy to say this or that."

I encourage you to use the word "easy" in all its forms—"easier," "less easy," "very easy," or "not too easy"—to invite ease into your life.

Whenever you feel anger rising, I also suggest laughing out loud—you'll quickly feel your mood shift.

If you'd like to experience this new concept, go immediately to page 138, exercise #3.

Enjoy the discovery! Freeing Oneself from Limiting Beliefs

Communication with Your Physical Body

Now that you have a better understanding of what divine responsibility entails, I want to help you absorb this fundamental concept by expanding on it. I will teach you how to integrate it by learning to communicate effectively with your physical body. Yes, you read that right! This may sound surprising; can you really imagine speaking out loud to a part of your body?

Let me tell you, it took a great deal of determination before I chose to do it. And believe me, the first time it happened, I made sure no one could see or hear me! Looking back now, I realize how much my body would have appreciated that healing dialogue long ago. This practice, which I consider miraculous, could have spared me many daily pains that had seemingly become permanent.

So I say it loud and clear: this new habit will improve your health and your life for the better. Remember, your body will always agree with you. As you learned in the previous chapter, your body is constantly listening to everything you say, do, and think. It trusts you and never questions whether the state of health it offers you is for your highest good. It simply carries out your conscious—and far too often unconscious— commands with complete neutrality.

You now understand that people become ill because they rely on highly destructive sources. At the same time, the most extraordinary aspect of life is that everything can be completely and easily transformed. I'll say it again: fatality exists only in human belief, not in the reality of the human being's creative power.

Here's the story of my first real experience with this sacred and revolutionary method. I broke a toe during an initiatory trip to Tunisia, where pride had clearly gotten the better of me. Two years went by, and I still had a small bump that remained quite visible on that toe. Whenever I wore closed shoes, my foot would go numb. It was uncomfortable, and I had grown tired of that sensation.

One day, I finally decided to speak to my toe. I looked around to make sure that no one could hear or see me talking to my body.

Here's what I said:

"I speak to you, my toe. I'm truly aware that I've been very prideful, and it's no longer necessary for you to cause me pain because I've received your messages."

Believe it or not, the small bump that had been there for two years suddenly began to shrink right before my eyes. It was truly impressive!

I still had to talk to it a few more times before the bump disappeared completely, because letting go of pride wasn't easy for me. You'll have gathered that when there's an issue with the toes, pride is strongly present within you.

After that revealing experience, I began to pay attention to everything that felt off in my body. As soon as I identified the source of any dysfunction, the pain would disappear, as if by magic.

The most important key to experiencing such healing is identifying the initial source of your pain. This is also the most difficult part to uncover. Your pain will persist until you do. Understand this: your body has always heard you, and it has responded to every word, action, and thought. The law of cause and effect has always been active in your body and your life. The more aware you are of this law, the faster it manifests.

It's important to be honest with yourself because you cannot lie to your physical body.

Unconsciously yet very naturally, the role of "savior" is often fully in place.

How many times a day do you think about your children, friends, or parents and start creating mental scenarios about what you could do to help them?

How many times have you said yes when your heart clearly said no? These are all points worth examining carefully.

How many times have you helped a particular person, and when you truly needed them, they answered yes gladly?

Probably not very often… maybe even never.

I'm almost certain you told yourself it would be the last time you ever helped them—that you were done!

And what happened the next time they asked for help?

Yes… You said yes, without even remembering those words you had thought, or perhaps even said out loud:

"This was the last time…!"

You know what might happen in your physical body? A sharp pain in the shoulder blades. This is a clear example of *self-betrayal*. If this happens to you, I strongly recommend speaking directly to your physical body and using energetic tools to release it quickly.

I often wondered how to find the initial source of a problem, because I knew that once I identified the source, the pain would go away. Sometimes, we're convinced we've identified the right source—but even after using all the tools, nothing works. Let me share an experience to help you understand what the *initial source* truly means.

When I was 15, I went for a car ride with my boyfriend and a girl I was doing a bilingual exchange with. Everything was going well until at an intersection, we were in an accident. While the injuries were minor, the shock was significant.

Years went by. After getting my driver's license, everything was perfect when *I* was the one driving. But whenever I had to sit in the passenger seat, or worse, in the back, I became extremely anxious. I absolutely *had* to keep my eyes on the road. I would glance to the side for just a second, then immediately snap my eyes back forward.

I did numerous healing sessions to free myself from this fear. I truly believed I had pinpointed the source of the accident when I was 15, and I worked on that specific memory for nearly 30 years. One day, while I was in France, I called a colleague who practiced a type of hypnosis and asked if we could have a session.

She used a pencil, asking me to follow it with my eyes for about a minute. Then she had me close my eyes and asked me what the true source of my car-related discomfort was.

To my great surprise, what came to my awareness was not the accident at 15, but an accident my *sister* had been in when I was around ten years old.

From that moment on, my fear of being in a car disappeared. I no longer had to watch the road anxiously. Yet all that time, I had truly believed I was working on the correct source.

Don't lose as many years as I did. If you speak to your body and it doesn't release a pain or symptom, dig deeper into your memories to uncover the *real* source.

As you already know, you cannot ask your body to regain or maintain perfect health if your words and thoughts are moving in the opposite direction. Consistency and awareness are absolutely essential if you want to achieve lasting results.

You cannot fool your physical body.

Remember, your body is simply responding to everything you say and think.

Try this consciously, and you will quickly witness the supreme intelligence of your body in action.

Through the love you show, you will experience remarkable and profound results—far beyond what you could have hoped for.

4

If you'd like to explore this new concept, go directly to page 139, exercise #4.

Enjoy the discovery! Learning to Speak to Your Physical Body

Bringing People Down from Their Pedestal

I've had the joy of welcoming people into my healing sessions and training who were over 80 years old. It made my heart so happy. These individuals had faith in themselves and could feel the benefits of the energetic tools in their physical bodies. It truly fascinated me.

There were two lovely women who made me laugh because, in the early years of my teaching, Master Saint-Germain was almost always present. To make him more accessible to everyone, I referred to him simply as *my uncle*.

Whenever these two women wanted an answer, they would always say:

"Madame Isabelle, could you ask your uncle if..."

I smiled every time, because the goal was to help everyone view him as an uncle or a beloved family member. That felt much more approachable than seeing this beautiful being of light placed high on a pedestal.

When someone is elevated in that way, others can start to feel less important and that is the very last thing the guides ever want.

These wonderful guides, each radiating such magnificent light, are fully aware that we, the humans, are the ones with physical bodies and the limitations we've chosen to carry. What they want is for us to look at ourselves with deep love, recognition, and pride for every step we've taken on this Earth and *never* to see them as more important than we are.

This brings me to speak about all the people in your life who, in your eyes, seem to be "above" you. The moment you believe that someone is more important than you, you are instantly diminishing and devaluing yourself.

To take back first place in your own life, it is truly essential to bring those people back down to your level. They are different from you, they've made different choices—but under no circumstances does that make them superior.

To even begin comparing yourself to someone else, you would need to have lived the *exact same life*, had the *same experiences*, the *same parents*, and gone through the *same karmic lessons*.

In other words, comparison is never valid.

You are *uniquely you*, and no one—not even the most enlightened being of light—is greater than you in essence.

Releasing Karmic Load

I can assure you that this current life is not always easy to carry, because before we incarnated, we *chose* to succeed where past incarnations of our souls had failed. We set the bar very high—because, in truth, this is our last opportunity to live on Earth under this ultra-limiting consciousness and transcend what continually pulls us into the trap of chasing power.

It is by recognizing and accepting that this craving for power arises from a massive illusion created by the controlling and directive mind, we will finally have the chance to free ourselves from this prison once and for all.

This leads us to the second mission that all human beings have on Earth: to release the karmic burden of the soul.

To fully succeed in this, it's crucial to understand what this concept really represents. You'll need to keep an open mind—because once again, this goes beyond typical human understanding.

Before explaining it further, ask yourself this:

How is it possible that you possess innate knowledge and skills in certain areas without ever studying them?

You might answer, "It's genetic—it comes from my parents, who were naturally gifted with their hands, for example." But... what if that's not the case? That's the real question.

To help you understand what I mean, I believe it's time for me to go into more detail about my life mission.

My soul made the bold choice to use the first 40 years of my life to experience and complete its unresolved life lessons. The goal? To completely release its karmic load and return it to zero point. I was asked to do all of this consciously, on my own, so I could later teach others how to do the same, clearly and effectively.

First, I had to live it out in my own physical body, so I could deeply understand every challenge—and most importantly, no longer feel the urge to repeat any of it. With the incarnation guide, I agreed that as soon as I crossed this threshold, there would be a drastic shift within my soul. We agreed that on my 40th birthday, my soul would return to the higher celestial realms and make way for a very old soul—one that would bring back the knowledge of Atlantean energetic tools and everything it had learned across its many incarnations.

Of course, I had no memory of this agreement... until the morning I woke up with a phenomenal amount of knowledge I hadn't had access to the day before.

Overnight, I became someone entirely different—with, as you can imagine, a deep urge to understand this paranormal phenomenon that had just entered my life.

There were no human guides to explain it to me.

I had to figure it out on my own. For years, every time I experienced something I couldn't trace back to a known cause, my guides taught me to ask myself three specific questions to determine whether what I was experiencing belonged to me, or if it was the return of a past life experience from my soul.

Here are the 3 questions I was taught to ask:

1. Did I say something?
2. Did I think something?
3. Did I do something?

Fortunately, I had a sharp memory and could easily scan through recent conversations, actions and thoughts.

If none of them matched my current experience, I would then ask to see what had happened in a past life that might be causing me to relive something in my present.

At that time, those were the only moments when I could access my clairvoyance and clairaudience.

The scenes appeared to me exactly as they had been experienced. I very quickly realized that if I could see the beings present in those visions, they could see me too.

I learned that I should approach them with utmost respect, gentleness, and never raise my voice.

Let's just say, at first, this new way of being was hard to adopt—I didn't yet have the necessary knowledge to do things "the right way."

But I learned quickly, because the consequences of my actions showed up in my daily life rapidly and with intensity. It wasn't easy to endure.

To truly understand a life lesson, ask yourself the three questions mentioned earlier.

Because until you are truly ready to hear yourself, your own thoughts, words, and actions—you will continue to create situations in your life that you'll likely not enjoy.

It is also important to know that in the energetic realm, everything is received literally and immediately.

Even if you say, *"I wasn't serious"* or *"It was just a joke,"* the consequences still follow. So why not make jokes that bring you great blessings instead?

There's an expression I've heard countless times:

"I take back what I said."

You need to understand that—even with good intentions—it's crucial to be clear and precise when you want to retract your words.

Ask specifically to neutralize the actual words you spoke, by renaming them, and you will see much better results.

There are many life lessons, and just like me, your soul met the guide of incarnation, who gave it the list of everything that would need to be brought back to a zero point during its next life on Earth. In past incarnations, the maximum number of lessons a soul would choose was four. It knew that going through these experiences would not be easy, as the initiation of a single lesson can last an entire lifetime before being truly understood and integrated.

Imagine a person who returns to reveal the lessons of violence, rape, oppression, and genetic manipulation. The first experience they face will be illness. For example, this can manifest as a rare disease, a physical or mental malformation, or body parts that do not develop in a just and perfect way. Most of the time, they will have chosen a family where violence is present from childhood, and where their parents belittle them by often making them feel that it's their fault if daily life doesn't go well. You now understand the complexity that karmic load brings into a life.

Now imagine everything I had to go through to truly release 44 life lessons in forty years of existence!

This leads me to discuss an important concept with you. For Earth to return to its original essence, certain souls chose to reincarnate on Gaia as representatives, as soon as the heart of humanity was ready to open to self-love. It was agreed that when this occurred, this group of souls (the representatives) would return to release the karmic burden of their soul family, their genealogy, and the collective from which they had evolved from life to life.

This teaching will certainly bring you a new and beneficial understanding if your path is filled with devastating experiences happening one after another without any rest.

These people have a true determination to face these challenges, but they often feel very alone and wonder what they could have done wrong to go through such an unpleasant life.

These people are around you. They need to understand what lies within them, as I had to do, so they can continue their mission while staying aligned with Love.

Accepting the experience of inhabiting their physical body and staying grounded on Earth is not easy for these individuals. They tend to escape into other dimensions, other vibratory planes, and many parts of themselves end up in the non-time—"a vibrational space where time does not exist." This temporarily allows them to avoid feeling physical pain, the limitations created by their human aspect, and especially to daydream and create a life full of illusions.

However, the undesirable effects that this brings to their physical body upon returning from this escape are a bit harder to endure. It starts with osteoarthritis, arthritis, and may eventually develop into fibromyalgia. It is therefore very important to understand that we are here on Earth to fully enjoy our existence, out of love for ourselves. To do this, it is essential to be well-grounded to the Earth and to inhabit our physical body at all times.

To those for whom this resonates, know that there is no fatality, because fortunately, your physical body carries supreme intelligence. As soon as you have truly accepted and acknowledged your divine responsibility, all you need to do is repeat this sincerely:

"I speak to you, my physical body. I realize that I have been hoping for a long time to free myself from this life of emotional suffering. I acknowledge that I have often fueled the desire to leave this Earth for a better world. I acknowledge that I have never realized that I am the most important person in my life and that I fully have the right to exist and to occupy a special place in my life and on Earth. My physical body, as I have received your messages, you no longer need to make me suffer."

You will immediately begin to feel the pain lessen. I invite you to realize that during all this time, you have been choosing to feed death instead of honoring life. Acknowledge and accept the fact that you created this period of great suffering, discomfort and illness caused by the law of cause and effect. The more you accept and acknowledge your divine responsibility fully, the more you will reclaim your creative power to love yourself and restore your perfect health.

Do not believe that everything is always easy. Beliefs, habits, and limitations are anchored so deeply in the different dimensions of the holistic body that very often, humans forget their new resolutions.

After doing tremendous work to speak lovingly to their bodies and vibrate in love for an extended period, and after experiencing a sense of well-being settling in, people revert to their old habits. They begin to feed the same patterns again—both consciously and unconsciously—and the physical body regains its pains.

Releasing karmic load requires a deep understanding of the holistic being, because there are so many spaces, places, vibratory planes, and dimensions to explore in order to release everything that has been experienced through your soul's past incarnations.

I invite you to look at the table of life lessons on **page #161**. Take the time to note everything you've gone through in your earthly life.

If you have more than four life lessons, it means you are a representative. You will therefore need to be accompanied by someone competent to proceed with this karmic release.

I invite you to book a session with me if needed. Above all, ask your soul if it is for your highest good.

Go to Appendix 1, page #161 for more details about the life lessons related to karmic load.

Embodying Your Divinity in Your Humanity

Many people believe they have such an important mission that they forget to live their true human lives. It is truly important to develop your senses and understand your life essence. At the same time, did you know that your divine dimension is already perfect? You don't need to go to great lengths to develop it further. You can simply choose to consciously awaken your divinity by embodying it in your daily life, in everything you do and are. It is essential that you learn to vibrate through your earthly life, fully anchored in the action of who you are.

For example, some people spend hours meditating in silence to find inner peace, but feel attacked as soon as noise surrounds them. They will often stop going to big stores, stop watching television, and refrain from doing many things because noise disturbs them. I would really like to say they are completely right to act that way, but I won't.

The truth is that we live on an Earth where sharing and exchange are an integral part of who we are and what we came here to experience. It is certainly not by isolating ourselves that we will regain balance in all things.

I would also like to draw your attention to an important point about this example: if external noise bothers you, be aware that it is the noise of your own thoughts that actually disturbs you.

If you wish to experience this new concept, go directly to page 144, exercise #5.

Enjoy the discovery! Learning to Speak to Your Human Self

The Importance of Living Life in the Present Moment

To understand what it means to live in the present moment, you must know and understand the impact of being in either the past or the future.

Let's begin with the past. Since you've been on Earth, you've experienced different events that have marked you, weakened you and transformed you. Very often, these experiences caused you to set aside your original personality (the one chosen before your incarnation) to develop a secondary personality that, in your opinion, better aligned with the expectations of your parents and society.

I'm willing to bet that this did not produce very good results. Since it's important to understand this concept clearly, here are a few examples.

Parents who wanted a boy but had a girl will, through their words and actions, make that child feel how disappointed they are. This little girl will develop pride at a very young age because she will feel the need to prove that she is just as efficient and strong as if she had been a boy. She will struggle to gain recognition from her parents, but her efforts will never be rewarded.

To be loved and accepted, she will develop a "tomboy" attitude in the way she dresses. She will do many things she never would have otherwise, such as carrying very heavy boxes. She will work very hard in school to succeed, but even after putting in all the effort, situations will always arise where her parents will make her feel she will never be the son they would have liked to have.

Throughout her entire life, this girl will keep trying, but her femininity will be repressed, and her relationship with men won't be easy either. In fact, until the last day of her parents' lives, she will continue to hope to someday hear them say they are proud of her 99% of the time, that will not happen unless she has done significant personal work to accept and recognize that she is an extraordinary woman and doesn't have to prove anything to be loved. She will have spent a large part of her life living in the past because the original source was her need to be loved by her parents. Emotional issues will arise, such as self-depreciation, self-devaluation, and a lack of confidence, faith, and love that will persist in her day and night.

Living in the future brings a lot of anxiety and anguish to many people. These emotions do not exist in the present moment. Living in the future prevents you from enjoying these moments with your children, your family, and the people you love. Since it's not possible to go back in time, one day you will realize your children have grown up, that you know very little about them, and you will begin to feel guilt and anger—and that will start another cycle of anxiety and anguish every time you hear that they are having problems.

Living in the present moment means making the most of the time we have to truly discover the person in front of us. It is a time for sharing and exchange. Your physical, moral, and emotional health will greatly benefit from it.

If you wish to experience this new concept, go directly to page: 145, exercise #6.

Enjoy the discovery! The Magnets of Your Humanity

PART ONE:
THE ISLAND OF ATLANTIS AND ITS TREASURES

In this part...

You will discover what the island of Atlantis and its treasures looked like in their original purity, long before the period of duality emerged, when everything was disrupted and self-destructed.

Here is the story of extraordinary people who knew how to live together, in perfect harmony, for many centuries.

Chapter 1: Introduction to the Island and Its Inhabitants

Did you know that everyone currently working in the fields of science, health, and research on Earth carries the memories of Atlantis? Indeed, this place was a very special island where all the great geniuses gathered to deepen their research, expand their knowledge, create devices intended for the accelerated regeneration of the physical body and update themselves in knowledge and enhancement of brain faculties. These devices were far more sophisticated than anything currently found in even the most well-equipped hospitals.

For a very long time, the Atlanteans served as models for all life on Earth. They were incredibly generous toward others, knowing that as long as Love radiated through the island's crystal, all would be well for everyone.

It was during this remarkable period that they created the energetic tools I use and teach today. These beings, passionate about the science of the human body, possessed highly developed senses that enabled them to see clearly into the future. This provided them with the extraordinary opportunity to validate all the impacts and accuracy of what they were creating in the present moment. Just imagine how precious such a gift was!

The rule on the island was simple: love for oneself was the priority. It's almost unthinkable to imagine that in such ancient times, people embodied the understanding that love had to resonate within and for themselves before being directed toward others.

I have visited Atlantis in meditation countless times. Each visit has helped me remember all these energetic tools. At first, I questioned the true purpose of all these visits. I was a very down-to-earth person who couldn't see, feel, or hear anything. You can imagine my surprise when I found out I was destined to teach how to work with the invisible.

At the very beginning, during my first visits to Atlantis, my eyes darted everywhere and I was in awe, like a child walking into a Toy's R Us! There were many large rooms, and each dazzled me because I felt like I was finally home. I knew what the devices were for and had fun experimenting with many of them. Sometimes I got instant results, and other times, nothing happened in my physical body.

You're probably wondering why?

I wondered the same thing and it took me a long time to understand. However, the answer was very simple. Some of these devices were made from materials that we don't have here on Earth. My body couldn't react properly to these unrecognized substances, as they would have done more harm than good. When I say "unrecognized," it simply means that these components did not originate from Earth. Since the body possesses an intelligence far greater than we can imagine, it has its own protective mechanisms. In fact, it instantly rejects anything that is not aligned with its highest good, and this manifests in various ways.

How wonderful it would be if everyone had the ability to understand how the physical body works. There would only be healthy individuals—or at least, people capable of using energetic tools to ensure their bodies always functioned optimally.

Now let's begin our overview of the island so you can deeply receive the vibrational image of this magical place. If you feel called to do so, I invite you to request the activation of your Atlantean cellular memories that lie dormant within your holistic being. That way, you will see, feel, and hear these powerful frequencies, and the knowledge they carry will gradually integrate more consciously into your daily life, one step at a time.

When people arrived on this majestic island, the first thing they discovered was a massive crystal guarded by four keepers. The role of these guardians was to radiate love for themselves. Through this activation of self-love, the guardians transmitted their sacred frequency to the crystal, which then supplied all the energy the island needed for electricity. Inspiring, isn't it!

Visitors accessed the island by boat, and upon arrival, all were required to present themselves before the crystal and meet the guardians. Each person had to place their hands and forehead on a facet of the crystal to energize and undergo a deep cleansing of their third eye chakra (located between the eyebrows). They remained in this position for a few moments and were then ready to follow the guide as they explored the island.

Depending on the purpose of their visit, some could tour the laboratories, the highly sophisticated devices, the scientists' quarters and the entire holistic medicine department. The visit lasted several days because there was so much to discover. Some visitors also came to the island for a complete health retreat—that is, for the heart, body, and mind.

The gaze of the Atlanteans was incredibly piercing, and visitors often felt "scanned" the moment their eyes met. However, the true purpose of this act was to establish a deep soul-to-soul connection. Their vibrations helped harmonize and soothe the visitors' nervous systems, which were often disrupted. This was done with the utmost respect and not as an intrusion into their bodies. Thanks to this act of kindness, it became much easier for them to regulate their nervous systems around the great electric-blue sphere. This was an important step for a deep sense of peace to settle in the core of their being.

Among the visitors, future students came to be assessed in terms of their senses, nervous systems, and vital energy. It's important to note that not everyone had the opportunity to study on the island, which is why they had to undergo various tests. These weren't written or aptitude tests but rather evaluations to determine their adaptability to a new environment. Since they had chosen to spend many years there without contact with their biological families, these new students were carefully tested and selected. The Atlanteans took great pride in ensuring the best experience for each of them.

Just like the students, it's important to recognize that everyone who lived on the island, whether to deepen their understanding of a field, a science, or simply to teach, were no longer in contact with their family members. You might think this was sad and that they experienced rejection and abandonment, but that was not the case. It was their destiny, and they felt very proud and grateful for it. This choice had been made consciously. When a family member was chosen, it was as joyous as winning the lottery. Moreover, the early days spent in Atlantis were devoted to learning how everything functioned, as it was quite different from anywhere else.

The island of Atlantis was regarded as a sacred place. It continuously emanated a vibration of love, which was the original source of everything that was created and developed across all domains. This is why everything said, thought, or done was precise, powerful, and resonated with absolute energy. This required a great deal of alignment at the heart level, as the Atlanteans understood that nothing could be taken for granted. Willpower and determination took on their full meaning.

The Atlanteans possessed highly developed faculties across all fields. Many concentration exercises, silent moments, attentive listening and observation were practiced daily with deep joy by both young and old alike.

They were very active, and everything they did had to respect the 7 Universal Laws that govern Earth: joy, love, sharing, respect, truth, justice and balance.

If you wish to experience this new concept, go directly to page 169, Appendix 2.

Enjoy your discovery! The 22 Universal Laws of the Multiverse

All these daily practices were known for their immense benefits, allowing the Atlanteans to engage their senses, mobility and emotions. They lived each day as if it were their last. Throughout their journey, they expressed sincere gratitude for everything they received. Gratitude was an integral part of their way of life.

Today, this word is rarely used. It's more often associated with those who follow a path of personal and spiritual growth, and these individuals are often seen as "enlightened." However, expressing gratitude for everything we are given on Earth is more than enough to be thankful to our Creator and to ourselves for understanding and applying the science of the spoken word to harvest beautiful seeds.

If you wish to experience this new concept, go directly to page 146, exercise #8.

Enjoy your discovery! Radiating Gratitude in Your Life

They also learned from a very young age to nurture everything beautiful within and around them. This made their hearts resonate with gratitude and pride for each of their accomplishments. The self-esteem of every Atlantean was maximized at all times. Vanity and ego did not exist in those ancient times, and fortunately so—because they would never have developed and achieved all they did otherwise.

Each person had a special way of moving around the island. Numerous stopping points were planned. People were naturally rejuvenated through sunlight, swimming, exercise, and healthy eating. There was no need for alcohol or tobacco to forget or rewind because stress was nonexistent. Natural fruit juices and plant-based beverages nourished their hearts, bodies, and minds. There was a great deal of beautiful color on their plates, and mealtime was a moment of gratitude toward the Source, God, Life in all things. What could be more wonderful than a plate that awakens the appetite just by looking at it! All the food they consumed was both delicious and nourishing. Their approach to food was very different from today. What they chose to eat was consumed purely for pleasure, not out of hunger.

In those ancient times, there were no issues related to body weight or digestion. *Prana* was their primary nourishment and represented the vibration of all that lived. It was through conscious breathing that the Atlanteans nourished themselves throughout the day.

These beings were very tall and slender, even taller than people on Earth today. Their gait was remarkable, with heads held high, shoulders pulled back and their gazes soft and directed forward. Their steps were firm yet light.

The air they breathed was also quite different, as it was continuously purified by numerous crystals arranged in a precise manner. Viewed from the sky, they formed a twelve-pointed star, and their vibrational rate was extremely high.

The island was vast, and part of its surface was devoted to agriculture. There were vegetable gardens that produced a wide variety of fruits, vegetables, and herbs.

Another large section of the island remained wild. The respect for nature and the hiking trails allowed visitors to recharge and inhale the various fragrances offered by the forest. Those who chose to study herbalism spent almost all their time in this area. They studied the different growth phases of plants and trees. The quality of the roots was particularly important as they were used to create many energy drinks offered to visitors. These were highly valued for both their benefits and their unique flavors.

Seed gathering was a very crucial activity. Seeds were utilized for planting in the Earth, and another portion was examined in laboratories to extract their primary substances. Many experiments and studies were then conducted to create medications with natural properties.

On this island of a thousand fragrances, numerous species of flowers also adorned the land. One of them—the poppy—was particularly precious for its essence. With its brilliant red hue, this small flower had significant healing properties. From its extracted essence, researchers were able to create a powerful antiviral. They believed that one day, Earth would need it. The researchers who attempted to create this antivirus would not be aligned with their hearts. That is why the information was transmitted to a human who could manifest the energetic antiviral capable of acting at the source and eliminating it. On the other hand, the emanation from the petals of the white rose helped anchor the work done energetically.

The trees were gigantic and served to protect the island from winds that often blew very strongly. Everything the Atlanteans needed to live was found on this precious island.

The houses in which the Atlanteans lived were mainly used for sleeping. Meals and activities took place in a single communal space. They had no need for material possessions like we do today.

During my early visits, I enjoyed experimenting with the devices, creating visualizations, or simply marveling at the multicolored light fountains. It was both magical and enchanting for my childlike heart!

Now imagine this vast space where the light fountains burst forth all around. These fountains served several purposes, and above all, they represented the light that gives life to all things. They did not shine in just one direction but in a continuous explosion. They were powered by precious stones, and the energy from these stones possessed healing and regenerative properties. Many energy tools were created from these stones.

When visitors came to the island, they spent a lot of time in front of the light fountains. They had to respect the natural order of things, as the benefits of the fountains varied depending on age, gender and height. Everyone began the journey at the same starting point, and the guides directed them toward the fountain corresponding to their specific needs. Some had a much denser emanation and were used to integrate what had been transmitted by the others. Children were especially drawn to the one that shimmered with a deep aqua blue. As soon as they saw it, their eyes would begin to sparkle.

These fountains also enhanced the precision of the senses. The more centered a person was in their heart, the more they were able to see, hear, and feel what was happening around them, across multiple vibrational planes simultaneously. The process unfolded gently and with respect for each person who came to drink in the energy of these fountains of light.

If you wish to experience this new concept, go immediately to page 147, Exercise #9.

Enjoy your discovery! The Fountains of Light

The Atlanteans did not age quickly. You might be surprised to learn that they maintained their childlike bodies for a long time. They all retained a much younger appearance and did everything necessary to avoid damaging their cells. Parents never fueled the need to see their babies grow up either. The present moment was the most precious teaching, and every second was the most wonderful. They consciously breathed in life and ensured it circulated throughout their holistic bodies at all times.

You've likely noticed that the days in Atlantis did not unfold the same way they do here on Earth. All these moments of pause to nourish their soul, heart, and mind replaced the robotic obligations of going to school or work.

Can you imagine if all human beings chose to do exactly what resonates in their heart with no financial obligation?

Chapter 2: The Atlantean Children

From the moment they came into the world, all babies were taken to the water, and it was pure wonder to see the newborns open their eyes in that crystalline space. They breathed naturally there.

Families shared the same home, with individual rooms for couples. All the children slept together, except for the newborns who remained in their parents' room for as long as they were breastfeeding.

The first year of life was crucial in Atlantis, and the couple participated in every stage of their baby's development to ensure the child fully integrated inner security, self-worth, encouragement and a sense of having a cherished place within the family. Parents communicated with their infant both telepathically and verbally. The development of the senses was an integral part of daily activities.

During this first year of life, they were able to detect whether the child would be more tactile or sensitive. This allowed the parents to naturally reinforce teachings related to the less dominant trait in their child. Gentleness, listening, sharing, experimenting, and communication were all elements of a healthy upbringing, and they took great pleasure in it.

The awareness of love ranked first among the values taught to children. These people knew very well that to create, manifest, and achieve what they needed for the island, everything had to originate from a vibration of love, for themselves and for everything around them. Without this state of being, the results would have been very different. Regardless of age, everyone shared the same goal: to reach the absolute in every area of their lives.

Among other values taught to children, trust, faith, determination and courage in oneself were highly encouraged. Unlike what often happens on Earth, the purity, innocence, and vulnerability of the Atlantean child were respected and nurtured throughout their lives. Thanks to the great respect for these qualities, the child developed a durable inner and outer security.

Their senses also developed rapidly due to their solid and unwavering foundation. The children never put themselves in danger because they could immediately sense what was right to do or not. They certainly never lacked in attention and even less in love, because, as you already know, that was the foundation of everything on the island.

The laughter of the children was very different from ours because it concealed no sadness, sorrow, or repressed anger. Their laughter radiated a light that spread far around them.

To preserve everyone's safety, communication was a central part of the educational process. Whether in word choice or sentence formulation, the Atlanteans used highly vibrant vocabulary. Negation was absent from their speech. When a sentence seemed ambiguous to an adult, they simply asked for clarification and the youth would rephrase. There were no expectations. The kinds of mental scenarios we create in our world today did not exist at that time because, in addition to verbal conversations, telepathy came first. Through telepathic communication, there were no emotions, no detours, no lies. The message was simple, true and precise.

I remember that very often, my daughter would speak to me and I would hear something different from the words coming out of her mouth. When I mentioned it to her, she would immediately respond, "Mom, get out of my head!" It made me laugh because she clearly understood that there was no need to lie or wrap her stories in anything. I've had that connection with her for a long time and it always delights me when I think of her and she calls me the next minute.

The precision of language was very important to them. It was their way of life, and everyone understood the law of return. Being highly aware of their thoughts and words, they already knew the outcome they would achieve.

Teaching young children the core values of the heart before teaching them to read or write was essential. Just as today, children model the behavior of their parents and the adults around them. It was therefore very important for the Atlanteans to embody the example of what they wished to see in their youth.

In the first phase of learning, all young children began by doing concentration exercises. In the beginning, parents would accompany their little ones. They would sit in front of something visually beautiful, like a flower. The child had to look at the flower until they could feel its texture, smell its fragrance, and become one with it. The time this took varied from child to child, and comparison had no place.

Each child was welcomed in their uniqueness, and there was no deadline to achieve this. This exercise was truly essential to their development. It helped them understand how to concentrate energy and direct it toward a single goal in order to manifest what they desired in their hearts.

Once the child succeeded, they would choose something even more complex, and gradually, they achieved perfect concentration. The final exercise involved water. At that stage, they could sense different types of fish, the depth of the water, and the presence within it, identifying them precisely.

Each Atlantean possessed a unique energetic signature, as well as a distinct category of fish or marine mammal.

This brings me to show you that idyllic part of the island where children would gather to discover and enjoy the benefits of water. Swimming and water play were very present in their lives. Through them, they developed perseverance and endurance. All the young ones were very proud and happy to experience this in a group. Sharing, encouraging, and helping each other came naturally to them all.

In that section of the island, floating docks could be seen at various distances from the shore. Some were meant for meditation, others for diving, and others for aquatic communication, depending on where they were in their learning journey. However, even the youngest used the diving platforms. The primary goal was to learn to let go and build self-confidence. The smile on their faces when they emerged from the water was a sight to behold. The more the children connected with the water, the faster their senses developed.

If you wish to experience this new concept, go immediately to page 148, Exercise #10.

If you wish to experience this new concept, go immediately to page 148, Exercise #10.

Enjoy your discovery! Liberation from the Dominant and Controlling Mind

Through concentration, the children connected with the different marine species and allowed themselves to merge with their energy. Over time, they became lighter, more fluid and more flexible. This energy of high-speed movement was the most anticipated moment, as all their limitations melted away like an ice cream cone in the sun. Many such exercises were practiced on the island because every means was perfect to reach their goals.

Communication with marine mammals was taught from a very young age. They had to learn to call upon the one they needed in order to descend into the ocean depths. They did so step by step. The development of underwater breathing helped to oxygenate their heart, body and different parts of their brain. Everything was an opportunity for learning.

The sensation of the underwater environment always brought greater precision to their movements. They used various warm or cold currents to propel themselves more swiftly toward their intended destination, day after day. Over time, their skin became increasingly firm and secreted a thin, greasy layer, allowing them to adapt to the temperature of the water. Their movements also became more and more fluid. There were many similarities with dolphin skin.

These little ones were a pure wonder to behold during training. Everything was designed so that the children would enjoy the experience. Rewards were not candies or video games, but rather additional practice of whatever the child most enjoyed doing. To ensure they were always willing and happy to learn, it was necessary to be attentive to their genuine needs and avoid overburdening them with activities they found more challenging. Learning began at a young age and never ended, because everything was a source of knowledge or understanding. Each child was expected to develop all of their faculties.

The responsibility of taking care of the younger ones was never an obligation for the older children. Instead, the joy of sharing their knowledge created a beautiful sense of gratitude in the heart of the one guiding the younger. This teamwork and sincere listening to one another unfolded quite naturally and without any hint of power or dominance.

The most fun part for the little ones was witnessing the manifestation of the energetic tools. When the manifestation process was complete, it looked like a real fireworks display of light. They all eagerly awaited this moment because it meant the creation had succeeded.

Some of the toddlers were assigned to stroll through the gardens and marvel at their beauty. Everything they were asked to do helped them grow on all levels—physically, psychologically, and emotionally. The activities offered were always a source of deep joy. Some stayed for just a few minutes, others for hours, not out of obligation, but simply for the pleasure of it. There was so much life on the island.

These young ones spent a lot of time playing outside. All the games encouraged the development of their faculties, mobility, flexibility, and dexterity.

Let me now take you to another specific section of the island dedicated exclusively to the education of children. There was a large building with several soundproofed rooms. As soon as the children entered, everything they touched emitted a sound. Without this sound design, the sounds would not have all been audible. Music was an integral part of their training from early childhood, hence the importance of these specialized rooms. It was essential that children develop their physical hearing as well as clairaudience. Numerous exercises were dedicated to this training.

Many majestic trees adorned the area, including three coconut palms that helped develop agility. The children had to climb to pick coconuts. Using a thread made from a material unknown to me, they had to wrap it around the coconut and pull it as tightly as they could. With this method, the coconut was sliced as easily as with a knife and it was much safer for them.

The building was also dedicated to precision training. It led to a more structured environment, better suited to developing concentration. What was truly magnificent to witness was the rainbow that manifested between the children's hearts. It was their way of saying hello each morning. The benefits of each ray nourished their subtle bodies and ensured a very high level of energy as well as perfect physical health. A large vegetable garden was located to the left of the building, allowing the children to learn all the steps needed to grow fruits, vegetables, and aromatic herbs with high vibrational energies. Each step was sacred, for everything was precious when it came to food, water, life, or the values of the heart.

They were also taught to love every little leaf, stem, root, flower, fruit and vegetable. The more they radiated love, the more they were filled with wonder at such abundance. They also experienced what happened when their consciousness was not aligned with the vibration of love. I don't need to specify that they understood the result immediately. A fruit that wasn't radiating love did not have the same taste, the same brightness, or even the same size. They all knew how important their participation was in the gardens, and they never failed to contribute their love.

Meditation was also part of their education. The heart, body and mind had to be in perfect symbiosis before adolescence. It was truly delightful to see the children engage in this daily practice. Unlike today in our schools, everything was tailored to them. They were very happy to learn because everything around them radiated love.

An open-air temple with large marble columns was dedicated to gratitude and giving thanks for everything they were given. This temple was situated near the children's building. Several times a day, people would visit it. This time of gathering was also part of their education. A constant state of grace emanated from these beings.

Raw materials also played an important role in the island's education. They used the earth and its components to develop touch and smell.

This created new materials by combining certain elements that would last over time.

Atlantean education was very rigorous, and this was for a very specific reason. Each person was expected to reach that space within themselves where the absolute would constantly vibrate—whether in confidence, sensation, vision, hearing, or faith. The consciousness of young Atlanteans was much more developed than that of today's youth.

Every question from the children received a clear, direct, and precise answer in the present moment. Adults transmitted knowledge with great precision, ensuring that the child understood the concept before moving on to the next one. When a question involved a process, in addition to explaining, they took time to give a physical demonstration so the child could integrate the information both visually and aurally. There were no limits to what the children could learn if it was dear to their hearts.

After each exercise, they took time for assimilation. They recalled their discoveries to embed them in both short and long-term memory. They repeated the same tasks as long as their bodies required. Integration into cellular memory had to occur until they felt that each step was inscribed in the core of the cell. Then, they would check with the Cellular Memory Specialists to ensure everything was correctly in place. These specialists used a sound device that could detect the difference between a saturated core and an incomplete one.

I've already explained that the first thing taught to children was concentration. The Atlanteans were well aware of the law of return. Because this was so important to them, they never hesitated to give their children the very best. Patience was regarded as a divine principle. This powerful vibration allowed them to remain centered in whatever they were doing in the present moment.

When I watched the young Atlanteans practicing concentration, it seemed so easy! That wasn't the case for me at all. They would regularly sit in front of a whiteboard and stare at it for about 3 minutes with their eyes open. Then they would close their eyes and remain that way for about 15 to 30 minutes. When they opened their eyes again, their gaze was radiant and their whole bodies seemed to emit a very peaceful glow. Thanks to this practice, their creative ideas became clearer and more precise. They would write them down to remember them for their future experiences.

The young ones also enjoyed moments of sharing with visitors, as they had the opportunity to learn about life beyond the island. Only a few Atlanteans were allowed to leave the island because the vibrational rate, lifestyle, and man-made laws did not align at all with the universal laws and energy present on the island. Nowadays, we would say that we're not living on the same planet. It was truly a world apart at that time.

Chapter 3: Studying and Working in Atlantis

On the island of Atlantis, there were many multi-story buildings and immense skyscrapers. Many of these structures were dedicated to understanding holistic health, studying and practicing, as well as conducting research on the human body.

Of all the buildings on the island, the Pavilion of Knowledge was my favorite. This was where the students' learning journeys began, regardless of the field they wished to study. In this pavilion, the training program placed great importance on developing the senses through concentration, experience and silence.

On the other side was the great electric blue sphere, where Atlanteans would go to regenerate the electrical systems of their nervous systems and brains.

Did you know that students progressed through each stage of their journey at an impressively fast pace? There was no room for self-sabotage in this process. The foundations of education were entirely focused on self-worth, accomplishment and success. Each person had their own program, and comparison was never part of the equation.

The goal was the same for everyone: understanding the full constitution of a human being—physically, psychologically, spiritually, energetically, emotionally—across all levels of consciousness, the unconscious and the supra-conscious.

When I speak of speed of accomplishment, it simply means that within a single Earth year, students would nearly reach all mastery in a field. Mastery consisted of perfectly knowing the associations and specific functioning of a specialty, whether physical or energetic. Once these understandings were integrated, the student received authorization to move on to a higher level.

On the island, everyone played a vital role. There was no hierarchical scale, and everyone had the opportunity to choose their profession in perfect harmony with the desires of their heart.

Learning took place over many years. There was no race against time. Everyone took the time needed to be in communion and reach the level of skill necessary for their future daily work.

All Atlanteans had the opportunity to become doctors if that was their deepest desire, as everyone was expected to learn the makeup of the holistic body. They knew very well that everything is interconnected and that the physical body and the energetic aspect are inseparable. This is why they were interested in plant medicine and manifested energetic tools. They treated both the physical and the energetic simultaneously. Balance in all things was essential to them, and they made it a point to honor it.

From their perspective, the notion of discipline was completely natural, as they understood the impact. It was a straightforward way of living. Honestly, I believe we would argue all day if we were asked to apply such a demanding way of life, day after day.

Some individuals developed their extrasensory abilities at the same pace—sight, hearing, feeling, smell, and taste. For others, it was completely different. For example, some began with the opening of clairvoyance or claircognizance. All Atlanteans had a record documenting their evolution. Once they reached a certain level, they had the opportunity to make their first career choice.

Later, after gaining sufficient experience in a particular field, they could choose to continue down that path or change direction. Everything was allowed and without obligation. The choice always belonged to the individual and not to their family.

As you know, children began working from a very young age. Remember, working for them did not have the same meaning as it does for us today. For instance, children would communicate with plants and flowers to discover their healing properties. These children had highly developed hearing. They would transmit this information to those who manifested energetic tools and to those who created elixirs, balms, creams, oils, medicines—everything used in medicine.

Women and men had the right to practice any trade they wished. A person's sex was not an issue for these people. In fact, for certain trades, it was even easier for the group to include both women and men. The seventh universal law of balance vibrated strongly in Atlantis.

In another building were kept the past and future memories of humanity. From these memories, the Atlanteans created devices that humanity would need to achieve "level three" healing of the physical body. These devices considered the natural mechanics of the physical body. Level "two" allowed for physical healing while combining an understanding of the source of dysfunctions. Finally, level "one" aimed to recognize the supreme intelligence of the physical body combined with the conscious understanding of the emotional dimension, so that self-healing could occur quickly.

It is important to understand that at level "one," when I speak of self-healing, this does not mean that recovery occurred in the same second, as several realizations are necessary to get there.

For example, the emotional recognition of all the words and thoughts that led the body to this state must be considered. Remember that everything starts with the self and returns to the self. We came to Earth to experience the law of cause and effect, which applies to everyone without exception.

The Atlanteans invented the artificial intelligence of the future. It was from this intelligence that they created various medical devices, some of which exist today on Earth. However, they invented others that are far more sophisticated, and the researchers and inventors currently on Earth must return to themselves, embracing self-love, self-respect, respect for others, and the truth of the heart in order to access all this information. That day is still a long way off, as humanity is only just beginning to awaken to consciousness. If they do invent these devices, it will mean that a large part of humanity will have returned to the self and acquired their creative healing power. That will be the most concrete proof we'll have of the power of love through the energetic tools of Atlantis.

I must admit that the tall buildings housing cellular and molecular regeneration devices fascinated me enormously. I went there many times, and each time, I was initiated into new experiences. In those moments, my heart and my eyes opened wide to everything that was presented to me, because it surpassed my human understanding.

At first, I thought I had a very active imagination that allowed me to go on such beautiful journeys in my thoughts. I believed that the time I spent exploring was my way of developing my senses! In that state of consciousness, everything happened very quickly, and I sometimes had the impression that I had been exploring for several hours. Yet, I realized that only 15 or 20 minutes of our earthly time had passed.

Still, I continued these journeys. Often, I would invite a friend to come along with me to discover this incredibly sophisticated medicine of the past. I later understood that it was actually the medicine of the future I was seeing and experiencing.

As I mentioned, the Atlanteans were very advanced in technology— far more than we are today. Sound technology allowed them to hear the vibrations emitted by an organ, a cell and an atom. Every part of the anatomy produced a distinct sound, and this technique opened the door to developing the devices of the future. Through this artificial intelligence, they were able to know everything that would happen on Earth. Based on this information, they began experimenting with different materials, waves, elements—everything they would need to create the medicine of the future. What you must understand is that, above all, they had to be in perfect alignment with the truth of their heart and in a state of absolute emotional neutrality.

If you wish to experience this new concept, go directly to page 149, exercise #11.

Enjoy your discovery! Being in absolute neutrality, returning to zero point.

You would have felt great joy watching them conduct their experiments. Everything was precious to them. They handled what they were going to use as if it were a newborn.

Unlike us humans, impatience never interfered with what they created, achieved, or manifested, because time held no importance for them. What they had to consider was their progression. Sometimes, if an experiment didn't go in the right direction, they would simply start over.

They took many visual and auditory notes. They didn't write anything down because they had photographic memories. The elements they assembled all had to vibrate at the same sound frequency, just like every part of anatomy and physiology, for that matter.

Their skill demonstrated perfect mastery of the matter. This is what made it possible to create the energetic tools I've been using for the past 20 years. Awareness of both physical and energetic logic has held a very important place for all inventors, researchers, and creators.

The work teams consisted of many members who took turns continuously. The results belonged to the group, not to a single person. Sometimes, they had to pause to discuss a problem, and after sharing their insights, they were able to continue by adding the missing elements or removing unnecessary components. Logic was very important to them, and the understanding of one complemented that of another.

Team spirit fueled their strength and determination. What they accomplished wasn't for themselves in the present moment, as they already had everything they needed. As mentioned earlier, what they created, developed, and designed was meant to serve future humanity.

Let's return to one of the soundproof rooms. Upon entering, all Atlanteans would state their name preceded by "I Am." By introducing themselves this way, a specific sound would be emitted and could be heard for several seconds. This unique sound aimed to assess the development of their extra-sensory abilities. The longer the sound lasted, the more developed their senses were. Once again, remember that there was no competition.

Chapter 4: The Training Rooms

Let's now explore the various training rooms. There was a building with five floors, one of which was dedicated to the senses and the anatomical parts related to each sense.

You could see all the parts of an eye, a nose, an ear and the skin. Everything was placed in jars made from a substance similar to glass, but not quite. They used vibrations from different crystals, such as quartz, brought to a very high temperature, to extract the essence. These jars were sealed and allowed the students to track their study progress.

Quartz allowed life to circulate at a much faster rate. Every little nerve reacted quickly, and they observed the reconstruction of an eye or another physical part related to one or more senses. Each step determined the next as everything developed just like a fetus in its mother's womb—but at a much quicker speed.

Their perspective was distinct, as they utilized both physical sight and etheric vision. Considering the physical body as a whole, they could identify which vibrational plane information was being lost and the cause of physical malfunction.

As soon as they received the information, they would regroup to get everyone's input. When everyone was in agreement, they made the necessary modifications. Often, they had to put their research in a state of neutrality. Based on their findings, they developed a new vibration to dissolve the barriers that prevented the natural circulation from flowing between planes.

Emotions were the primary source of these dysfunctions. They had to consider the root cause or the original experience that triggered the issue.

They needed to ensure that it was fully released before reconnecting the missing pathway. Don't think everything was easy—some emotions caused the same type of energetic blockage, and sometimes it took several attempts to restore the original perfection.

The Atlanteans were well aware that everything begins and ends with oneself. In doing these experiments, they had to understand how the human brain functioned across its different evolutionary stages.

This means that all these energetic tools and highly sophisticated devices had to be adapted to each human era. That's why they took their time, never rushing. They lived through all these evolutionary eras when they had even more time, because their knowledge and skills weren't yet useful. Still, the stakes were high because everything they created in terms of technology would serve different future civilizations.

Communication between the brain and the various parts of the holistic body had to be extremely fluid—especially on Earth, where we've returned to release the impact of the entire experience of duality. Among many life lessons, it's genetic manipulation that has caused the most dysfunction in the brain. Therefore, it is vital to understand the impact this can have on the entire physical body.

Can you imagine a 3D translucent brain in which you can observe the tiniest cells, all the information relays, neurons, and each compartment managing different parts of the body? The Atlanteans had this vision, which is why they could understand the function of every aspect of anatomy and physiology.

I now invite you to visit the building dedicated to research. On the island, all the buildings used for learning, research, design, and education stood side by side in a crescent shape. At the center was the pavilion dedicated to children.

Several guides were stationed at the entrance of the research building to direct newcomers to the right place. There were many rooms, one of which housed the results of all their research. These guides accompanied visitors to answer their questions and ensure nothing was overlooked.

You could see many researchers working alongside young Atlanteans. Their complementarity meant that their discoveries were always the result of a team working in constant symbiosis. Through their innocence and keen senses, the young Atlanteans had a talent for quickly understanding and analyzing the different elements involved in research. It was important never to take the past for granted, as previous research might have yielded excellent results—or none at all. This meant that every time they started a new research project, they always began from scratch, without relying on what had already been discovered.

In this research building, there was also a room dedicated to the development of memory. Every day, researchers spent time studying how memory functioned. Their goal was to organize information by importance and chronology for each discovery. Remember, it was the children who manifested the energetic tools. As soon as the researchers discovered new information about memory, the children would immediately create a new sacred tool and rush to test it with the researchers. Sometimes the children had to test different energetic tools before achieving the desired results. In fact, it was through memory that they discovered time-spaces, time corridors, and a chamber of time's incompressibility.

For decades, young Atlanteans closely observed the visitors. As soon as they focused their awareness to a part of the physical body, they could perceive the various vibrational planes and dimensions. Some of them, who had different perceptions, could see both inside and outside of an organ, a cell, or a blood cell—every part of the physical and etheric anatomy. For others, vision was more limited. However, even without perceiving all these dimensions and vibrational planes, they instinctively knew when an anomaly was present and could even pinpoint its location in the physical or etheric body. This group possessed claircognizance. In other words, they simply *knew*. These groups of young people often worked in teams because they liked to validate the information they received before sharing it with visitors.

Studies and research conducted in the laboratories were cataloged in physical files and also transmitted to the artificial intelligence of the future that they had created. They knew that a day would come when human beings would sufficiently develop their senses to access it. I know it's not necessarily easy to understand that your soul has lived through several incarnations before your birth and that everything it has experienced is recorded within you. The more you return to love for yourself, the more these sacred pieces of information will become accessible to your conscious awareness.

Let us now explore the building dedicated to medicine. This is where I found myself during my meditations and time-traveling visits to the island. Upon arriving at this place, I was welcomed by several guides. One day, I was in a room with many Specialists and one of them asked me to follow him. He led me to one of the entrance doors. Above the door was a large board listing the names of people currently incarnated on Earth who have the mission of transmitting knowledge. It was a great surprise to me when I saw my name on the board in second position. I thought it couldn't be possible. I truly believed I had a vivid imagination! However, I can now affirm that I wasn't dreaming, as I have taught more than 19 different training sessions on all the energetic tools. I even created a powerful program with 153 videos to better understand how the holistic body functions, how to use these sacred tools, and to receive a treatment at the same time. This series of 153 energy treatments, derived from the sacred tools of Atlantis, is simply exceptional and unmatched in power.

Let's now head to the second floor of this building to discover some of the devices specifically designed for healing the physical and multidimensional human body. In the first room, all the devices are used to check blood pressure, perform blood tests, conduct dialysis, as well as to analyze different human and animal blood types. These studies would become useful on the day when a person is bitten by a rabid animal. Remember, thanks to artificial intelligence, the Atlanteans had access to the future.

In another room, there were devices capable of scanning a system, an organ, or the entire physical body. I really enjoyed experimenting with these devices. One of them was a bed one had to lie down on. This device scans from the feet upward to the head, performing a full reading of the physical body and printing the results similar to a card reader. As it moved back down, it made certain corrections to what had been disqualified. Another report contained the data of what could not be corrected during the healing session, along with explanations. Thanks to the results revealed in this valuable report, the doctor could inform their client of what they needed to understand and accept before the next visit if they wished for the correction to be complete.

Several devices were made of light jets. Depending on the person's issues, the treatment often ended with one of these devices to seal the work done on the physical and energetic levels. Sometimes, clients had to first sit under the light jets before moving on to the other devices. This process prepared them adequately to receive frequencies with a much higher vibrational rate than their physical bodies. It is important to understand that as soon as discomfort or illness manifests in the holistic body, the vibrational rate decreases.

In another room, we found devices used to develop and repair discordant cells. As you already know, in Atlantis, they never removed any part of the physical body. The body was treated from the source cells and reconstructed. However, they knew that one day humans would undergo surgeries. So they also made sure to design everything crucial regarding this process. On the other side, there was a much more spacious room, which was used for the necessary adjustments of the senses. Each device emitted a specific sound when the right vibrational and sonic frequency was reached. In this room, large screens projected a 3D internal and external image of a sensory organ. One function allowed the separation of each part to easily detect malfunctions. What was infinitely small became magnified and I could say that a kind of microscope was part of almost every device.

The most intriguing room for me was the one dedicated to the brains. Even today, I am still fascinated by the complexity of its functions, structure, and all the information relays it contains. I can compare the brain to a computer. There are many programs, interfaces, compartments, memories and hidden information from realms unknown to today's researchers. Viewing the inside of a brain with the kinds of devices found in Atlantis would probably be the most wonderful gift we could offer neurologists. However, for designers and researchers on Earth to access all this technology, they need to activate the Sacred Radiance of their heart and learn to observe beyond what their human eyes can see.

During one of my meditations in Atlantis, I entered another room filled with several devices and distinct chairs. Naturally, I wanted to experience their benefits and found myself in a funny position. Sometimes I was standing upright, sometimes upside down with my feet in the air, and sometimes lying down in a way that allowed me to see the ground. When my experience ended, I immediately asked what all these chairs were for. The answer was surprising! These different positions allowed for the calibration of blood in the physical body. To understand better, they acted directly on the arteries and veins that were blocked. It's fascinating to know that a sound wave can unblock what reduces blood flow and prevents proper circulation. Isn't it amazing to know that everything is possible?

Chapter 5: The Solar Installations

Let us now explore another part of the island where the solar installations were located—they powered the electrical circuits were not energized by crystals.

To help you visualize, they resembled the solar panels we currently have on Earth. However, they were made from substances extracted from the essence of crystals, much like the containers used for the various anatomical parts under study. Metals such as iron and aluminum were not their raw materials. What they invented had to remain functional for decades and decades. Researchers and creators often collaborated, which is why they shared the same pavilion.

Before going any further, it's important to understand that the process of extracting the primary source of a crystal was carried out simultaneously with the regeneration of the used crystals. This ensured that life circulated in all things at all times. It was a true marvel to witness this process in action. Vibrations in various hues emanated from the crystals, like a sound-and-light show. This section of the pavilion was accessible to visitors.

The structure housing these solar panels formed a rectangle. A process allowed them to use only the energy they needed without limitation. They never wasted energy and always optimized usage to ensure everything remained in harmony at all times. Several solar panels were activated for upcoming constructions, devices, and any other electrically powered processes. They were very forward-thinking, and remember that, through the artificial intelligence of the future, they always knew what needed to be created.

In this part of the island, access was quite limited. Only specialists were allowed to enter for numerous inspections, and it could be said that safety was the top priority. Even the clothing they wore was adapted to the vibrational field, which emitted powerful waves continuously. However, the energy was concentrated to spread precisely where the need was confirmed. Honestly, if everything operated this way today, there would be no workplace accidents. Quantity was never the priority on the island—quality was.

This is also why they took multiple breaks throughout the day to maintain lightness in their thoughts and to ensure their physical bodies remained energized.

Chapter 6: Atlantis Underwater

As I reflect on all the dazzling journeys I've taken to Atlantis, I remember a particular day when I accompanied some of my students to explore the underwater part of the island.

I now invite you to take this journey with me. Are you in? I suggest you sit comfortably. Let your thoughts drift without trying to control them. Don't even try to imagine what I'm going to share with you—instead, simply invite the energy of Atlantis to awaken the dormant memories within you.

On this guided journey, we began by visiting the Grand Crystal, where the guardians of the island dwell. Each person in the group was asked to perform the ritual of placing their hands and third eye on the vibrant, magnificent crystal for a few minutes. Once everyone felt aligned and energized, we followed the magical path leading to the underwater platforms, which required us to cross half the island. The path was paved with beautiful small gemstones. The further we walked, the more we became aware of the importance of anchoring ourselves deeply to Gaia, the Earth, and of breathing in each moment spent on the island, with love for ourselves.

The guides made us feel the vital importance of our roles in the vibrational transition of Earth, which has already been underway for several years. They spoke to us telepathically, directly to our hearts. Each person received the vibrational message that was just right for them in that moment.

When we reached the first platform, the guides explained that we would be swimming through a very special corridor. It had been specifically designed to allow our eyes to see clearly underwater and to breathe comfortably. Once everyone was ready, we dove in together, and I must say, the experience inside was absolutely magical. To start with, a deep calm and peace settled in our minds, and our heartbeats began to slow down.

It became simple and natural for us to descend into the depths. At 50 meters below the surface, our eyes filled with awe as we caught a glimpse of a golden structure resembling the Tree of Life. It was breathtaking! However, the guides gently and lovingly informed us that we would not be able to access these installations. They also explained that our eyes were unprepared to see the true reality of this place—veils of invisibility prevented us from perceiving the actual appearance of the spheres.

We learned that these structures were created to experiment with the power of their medical, cosmo-telluric, and astronomical devices. Because they utilized a variety of substances, this site was protected against all forms of explosion and radiation. One of the spheres was used for the self-destruction of unused matter, as the Atlanteans never kept outdated prototypes. They were always moving toward better technologies.

Beneath the waters lay many varied structures, each serving a distinct purpose. Several were dedicated to the study and experimentation of different marine substances. We were told that everything found in the ocean's depths could be combined to create powerful new materials with no expiration date. These materials were used to construct the island's buildings. Everything they built followed the golden ratio.

We then moved toward a cave with exceptional energy-amplifying properties. When researchers needed to test the quality of a new substance, they brought it to the lab. A very small amount was placed in a hermetically sealed container and left to absorb the cave's energetic properties for several hours before being reanalyzed. They quickly realized this energy was a gift from the heavens. It has remained untouched to this day. They knew better than to remove any particles, as the site's unique vibration would instantly shift.

The Atlanteans possessed absolute discernment. They co-created everything humanity would ultimately need. Their sense of duty was unshakable during those sacred times. Water remained their most precious treasure, as everything it contained was a source of life and abundance.

Our visit continued to the farthest platform from the island. The guide explained that it had been built for the purpose of teaching about the ocean's depths. The youth had constant access to this area. By diving from here, they would enter the "Informational Structure." It was named as such because the young Atlanteans could feel the vibrations of every marine mammal, fish, crustacean, sea serpent, and more. Understanding it all was crucial for them, as this allowed them to make eco-molecular associations.

Because they respected the ocean, they ensured that all life forms reproduced in a fair and balance manner at all times. The children were fascinated by the marine creatures. Within this structure, a walkway connected one sphere to another, and it was sensitive to sound. Every sound made by an approaching entity was detected, calibrated and harmonized in real time. The information was stored in both short- and long-term memory as well as in felt experience.

Their learning techniques were adapted for each Atlantean. The primary goal was to capture the interest of the young so they would enjoy learning, feeling, hearing, and seeing beyond all perception. At first glance, it might have seemed demanding, but in the end, we learned that everything was done with deep respect for each individual. Just like on Earth, when a child is excited to participate in an activity, they are more receptive than one who does it out of obligation, without joy or interest.

It was truly fascinating to watch these young geniuses at work, whether in the underwater structures or in the pavilion dedicated to them. These prodigious children shared a common radiance of wonder emanating from their entire being. It was extraordinarily beautiful to behold! The further a child progressed on their path of evolution, the more colors were included in their aura. The shades of blue captivated me. I learned that as the child developed their oral and telepathic communication, the more diverse the blue hues within their glow became.

When a group of children gathered on a walkway, none of them dove in. We observed that they breathed deeply, gently descended into the water, and took their time to gradually immerse themselves until their entire bodies were submerged. Then, we had the privilege of witnessing a magical ritual unfold before our dazzled eyes. In a burst of joy and deep communion, each one focused their attention on their heart to thank the ocean depths for welcoming them and teaching them how to honor all forms of life. In this radiant state of love, the young ones began to perform graceful circular movements. Schools of fish emerged from all around and danced in the center in response to their offering. What beauty—it was majestic!

When they had finished, they made their way to the entrance of the building. A door opened and closed behind them. The water withdrew on its own. At that moment, another door opened to welcome them. Each child had the opportunity to choose their preferred learning sphere of their choice. On some days, they stayed there for hours. The vibrational level was always so high that fatigue never set in.

We noticed that in one of the spheres, a child was seated in front of multiple wave and frequency sensors visible on several devices. Through thought alone, he made a specific object and its full composition appear on a large screen. This child had the ability to reproduce everything he had seen, felt, or heard. It was impressive! He used a set of selective cells[1] in his brain to record everything. Another set of selective cells allowed him to perfectly reproduce everything he needed for his projects, research, and creations.

In another sphere, a small group of children was busy transmitting information telepathically among themselves. This way, they developed their teamwork skills, as sometimes they went underwater specifically to relay important information to others inside the sphere.

---

[1] In the book *The Life and Teachings of the Masters of the Far East*, there is mention of these selective cells in the section on the faculties of the brain.

They regularly switched places. Once a child had mastered telepathy completely, they no longer needed to perform those exercises. The same applied to all other senses. While learning crucial steps in their development, they never forced anything. Quite the contrary—they lived these experiences fully anchored in the present moment.

At the end of each day, they would all go to one of the sound chambers on the island to validate the work they had done that day. In fact, the guides taught us that toddlers were only allowed to begin exercises inside the spheres once they had fully assimilated and validated the learning stage related to concentration within that sound chamber. Generally, this process took a few years.

We also observed that many spheres within the youth learning structure were empty and were reserved for future use. At first glance, one of them appeared empty, but we were surprised to find it was actually filled with a substance I would describe as gelatinous. This material was used for primary cellular and molecular regeneration. When an experiment yielded inconclusive results, they placed the failed creation in this room, and within moments, it returned to its original state. Fabulous, isn't it? This meant they could redo their experiments as often as they liked without ever wasting energy or materials.

When their day came to an end, a small ritual of gratitude would take place. They returned to the water and spun around for a few moments in one direction, then in the other. They repositioned themselves into a circle and once again radiated love as a sign of thanks. This ritual allowed them to integrate the work done throughout the day. Sometimes, they swam back to the shore, and other times, they used the platforms to return to the island.

Every evening, families would gather to share the information from their day. Parents and children alike enjoyed these moments with such joy in their hearts. Each person spoke in turn, and they respected the speaker until the end of their sharing, without interrupting. Pride could be seen in everyone's eyes. When the sharing ended, the families would complete their health routine before going to sleep.

At that time, they were already aware of wastewater recovery because everything was transformed and served another purpose. For example, the water used for washing was repurposed to nourish the plants, trees and gardens. They filtered the water using various corals and precious stones, whose primary properties served to neutralize and transform matter. They had installed both indoor and outdoor water piping systems. Once again, everything was in balance.

The last part of our visit took place in an underwater structure designed for the researchers. Just like the young ones, the adults also had their rituals of gratitude, thankfulness, and integration. They gently entered the water, which allowed them to advance their research. After taking a precious moment to give thanks, they headed to their structure. There were many more of them than the young ones, and as soon as they entered, each would go directly to the sphere that corresponded to them. Almost all were occupied. However, we observed that when they succeeded in manifesting the outcome of their research, they went to the sphere located at the end of the structure to begin their functionality tests.

They also had a gelatinous-looking sphere similar to that of the young person. For them, each sphere had to be impeccably clean.

In one of the spheres, the team of researchers communicated with the young ones who manifested the energetic tools. These children were studying plankton in all its forms. Food was the primary source of life for many species. Their studies led them to a better understanding of the systems of mutation, and cellular and molecular multiplication, based on the location and constitution of the plankton being studied.

Remember that life in all things was their priority. From the results obtained, they knew how to reproduce the vibrations that enabled the creation of various materials they used on the island. Reproduction was always ensured, and they remained committed to preserving the marine environment intact at all times.

The researcher sphere that impressed me the most was the one for finalized products. Each of the prototypes physically existed on the island, but in this sphere, all the stages of composition would appear on a screen, and the entire process was documented from "A to Z." When everything was completed, the image appeared in 3D. They used programming codes that were different from those we use today, though still somewhat similar. Everything created in the material world had to be calibrated to the correct vibrational and sound frequency. This step took more time to achieve than all the other steps combined.

All the spheres within the underwater structures shared common features, such as components, sound waves, and cellular and molecular binding agents that had been used to build them. The Atlanteans assembled the structures directly in the water, piece by piece. They had a very advanced mastery of gravity, which made it easy for them to ensure that all these spheres remained very light. This was particularly useful for handling and installation.

What you need to know to understand that I am not contradicting myself in my writings is this: during my meditative journeys to Atlantis, I could only see the external underwater structures. However, while I write, I can see everything with precision because they are giving me all the access I need. There are no veils of invisibility.

It was important for me to clarify this point.

Chapter 7: The Birth of the Energetic Tools

As you know, it was the children who first thought to create these tools. Initially, it was only to help a visitor troubled by swirling thoughts in their mind.

These children had a remarkable understanding of what emanated from each person and each thing. They also possessed knowledge of the holistic body functions.

Their vision was so developed that they could discern different vibrational planes. They quickly learned to identify the root cause of a problem by observing the one and only cell that vibrated differently and held very distinct properties from the others. They understood that by treating the discordant cell directly, the healing process would activate very quickly.

A group of young individuals was particularly gifted in this field, as they not only experimented with their discoveries but also explained everything they were going to do in an energetic and step by step manner. The visitors appreciated knowing the process before receiving a treatment. From that point on, the first thing they did before performing a treatment—or if you prefer, an energy healing—was to find the source cell. As soon as they found it, they would pour the prepared elixir into the center of the cell. Then, they would project white rose petals to fix the source. In the following seconds, the cell would recode the other cells and healing would occur very quickly.

They developed several elixirs because the cells did not always respond positively. Since the children knew that emotional imbalance was the primary source of dysfunction in the physical body, they had designed a repertoire of different emotions. Over time, their list became very extensive. They quickly realized why there were so many flowers and plants around them. Everything had been planned!

The children who worked to create the energetic tools loved demonstrating their latest discoveries to the adults. They were very proud of the final results. From that moment on, the cultivation and study of plant properties entered a whole new dimension. The young ones never tired of their experiments. Their favorite part was interacting with the visitors. Smiles formed quickly when they saw the transformation process occur on the cellular and molecular level. They knew they were on the right path when healing took place.

As soon as a child begins training to become one of the island's Specialists, all hearts vibrate in unison to support and accompany that child for many years.

To create the tools, the children began by calling upon Gaia, the Earth and the Cosmos to unite these two powerful, complementary vibrations that constitute the universal manifestation plane. By combining these two energies, they could easily release human emotional patterns as well as those inscribed in the various components of the holistic body. After many experiments, they created the spiral tool. Each spiral had a different function and intention

The universal manifestation plane is the space where the resonance of words and thoughts always returns to the one who expressed them. It was essential to unite these two energies because there is always the human part and the energetic part to consider in order to maintain balance. When the children presented their energetic tools to the adults, a deep joy emanated across the island. They knew that thanks to these tools, the entire emotional dimension could be released, allowing peace to settle again in the human being.

When the young ones in Atlantis manifested the ejector spirals, they took a significant time to conclude that these would be the ideal tools for releasing emotions and unspoken words. The spirals activate from the Earth and, as they spin, can reach even the most closed-off places of the holistic being, acting like magnets. Humans often fear loss and resist heavily, which is why it must be done repeatedly until one is willing to let everything go. It is always better to speak your truth in the moment rather than repress it, even if you're afraid of hurting someone or saying the wrong thing. At first, you may feel a little awkward, but over time, you'll manage to be heard. Repressed emotions can lead to colds, flu, and a weakened respiratory system.

In studying how visitors functioned, they noticed that one person's emotional state could affect others. This created confusion in the nervous system. That's when the children understood what it truly meant to be empathic. Unlike what we are currently taught on Earth, empathy does not mean feeling compassion for others. It rather means feeling the other's physical, emotional and psychological pain in your own physical body. Since the spiral technique worked so well, they decided to create another spiral specifically for this type of release.

Sometimes, the children engaged in an energetic reading in the morning with the visitors, and they noticed small particles—better known as miasmas or astral debris—clinging to their astral bodies. They explained that during sleep, the astral body leaves the physical body and travels to different vibrational planes to receive teachings, recall knowledge, or simply visit an incredibly beautiful garden of light. However, when someone sleeps and doesn't feel well within themselves, they might end up in vibrational planes with less beautiful energy, and such energies can attach to their astral body. These young prodigies then created another spiral to release these disqualified energies from the entire holistic being of the visitors.

The children greatly enjoyed experimenting with their energetic tools, as even though the visitors couldn't see the spiral with their human eyes, they felt the benefits in their physical bodies, and a sensation like a whirlwind occurred inside them.

Over time, the children studied the properties of stones and minerals and created energetic tools that embodied their attributes. For example, the violet energy balls were manifested from amethyst, which facilitates the transformation and transmutation of disqualified energy.

Thus, they manifested balls of light, spirals, balms, powders, elixirs, spheres, etc., to care for the holistic body. They also created energetic tools for water, the Earth, the Cosmos, birds, animal food, and plants.

Chapter 8: The Children of Today

As you've seen, the life of the Atlanteans bore no resemblance to what we know here on Earth. On this fabulous island, everything that was done, thought, or experienced had one single and unique goal: to respect creation in every way.

When I spoke to you about the education of children or the way these beings with highly developed mystical powers behaved, you noticed that it had nothing to do with the practices of today, where the energy of power pervades everything that is experienced. However, all human beings are called to return to the source of the Original Sacred, which is accessible at any time. The only non-negotiable condition is detachment from serving one's own needs. Everything must be done for the greatest good of all.

The will to serve and the determination to accomplish what is dear to your heart are compatible. What is not compatible is the desire to appropriate knowledge, wisdom, a place, or even a person—such as your children. Everything has been placed in service to humanity, and there is enough abundance for everyone to eat their fill. The energy of money has divided humanity. When we attempt to eliminate money to create another system of exchange, we end up back at square one once again. There was a time in Atlantis when each person contributed according to their abilities and interests. Everything was balanced. No salary was necessary. Everything was available to everyone.

Excess is still very present on Earth. Being naturally curious, I'd like to know: Does always wanting more make you happier? Are you in good physical, emotional, and psychological health because of it? Are you beginning to understand the importance of today's children? Let me explain.

Did you know that there are thirty-two different families of children incarnated on Earth? Each one has its own characteristics, its own energetic tools, and a significant role in the transformation of the Earth. Know that they are much more advanced than us, the parents, in many areas. They did not incarnate on Earth to learn algebra, but rather to remember their original identity and to reactivate their cellular memories.

Did you know that the knowledge of Atlantis is a part of them, and that the day they recover their energetic tools, life on Earth will change? I understand that most of you reading these pages probably won't understand what I'm referring to, and that's perfectly normal. I'll be happy to help you uncover it.

Honestly, have you ever thought of your children as lazy or lacking intelligence because they're disinterested in school? I'm happy to tell you that this is far from the truth. Your young ones are far more advanced than the material they learn in school. I suggest you immediately stop underestimating them and start genuinely showing interest in them. I encourage you to take the time to ask them what they're passionate about and what they would like to do with their days. If you're ready to listen, you'll probably make extraordinary discoveries about them. You'll be amazed to see how much more they can teach you than you could ever imagine, even in your wildest dreams.

In today's world, I want to draw your attention to the fact that children are under the influence of emotional programming. Emotional blackmail is part of their upbringing. The lack of quality presence from parents is common. Teachers and parents look for someone to blame when a child, feeling the need to get attention, acts out. A little more listening, respect, and consideration would be very welcome. To learn more about the thirty-two families, I invite you to visit my brand-new website: https://isabellestgermain.com

PART TWO:
THE KNOWLEDGE OF
SACRED ENERGETIC TOOLS

In this second part...

I will explain in my journey in more detail, covering the different phases involved in the materialization of the sacred tools, as well as the energy healing techniques I have been using for the past 20 years. I will also teach you about the remarkable characteristics of each one. Thanks to these tools, you will undoubtedly experience profound and beautiful transformations in your daily life.

Chapter 1: My First Steps and Discoveries

As you already know, I have never met a single human being capable of teaching me or explaining what had occurred within me since that irreversible change at the level of my soul. I can assure you that, even 20 years later, this remains the case.

I've always wondered how this event could have taken place, because during the first 40 years of my life, I was neither naïve nor a sheep. I was more like a warrior who went through numerous experiences and remained standing despite feeling completely overwhelmed by what was happening to me.

I admit I probably didn't read the fine print of my life plan before coming to Earth because there likely would have been major edits to make! But here I am, and I dare to believe that this change was for my greatest good.

At the very beginning of this metamorphosis that occurred for me, I was eager to share the knowledge, and I was so happy to have this role to play in the circle of life.

I quickly realized that there weren't many people ready to accept and recognize the creative power of Love or see their reflection in the mirror as the greatest wonder in the world. I had no idea I would disturb so many people. I have always worked with humility and simplicity, offering as much as I can to those around me. However, I had to respect human beliefs. I must admit that my journey wasn't as thrilling as I expected. After all these years, I had to stay the course. Many times, I have told myself that humanity is far from understanding just how easy and pleasant life becomes when we realize it's simply about living each experience without judging it. The Earth's transformation process would happen so quickly under those conditions.

I was greatly mistaken because humans are comfortable in their old shoes. Most people cling stubbornly to their beliefs, which often keep them at the bottom of the barrel. They continue to pray to the heavens, hoping to be heard and receive help. When help does arrive for these individuals, they often refuse to receive it. They expect assistance to come only from the sky. Between you and me, it is essential to ask in order to receive, but it's also important to accept the help that shows up every time.

Twenty years ago, it was complicated in a certain way because everything seemed to come from nowhere, and I had the feeling that humans thought the exact opposite of the information I was receiving. I had to develop great faith and trust, as I often wanted to stop teaching.

Through this knowledge that resurfaced in my consciousness, I discovered the complexity of the different dimensions, parts, aspects, and personalities of the being that operate on different vibrational planes. I often asked myself how humanity would manage to restore order if all these details were not revealed.

You'll understand that the answer was very simple: "You just have to teach the knowledge you carry within, and you will see that more and more people will want to understand and put your teachings into practice." So, I chose to continue along this wonderful path despite my initial apprehensions.

The First Months

During the first months of experimentation, I noticed many changes taking place within me. I was becoming increasingly gentle, more attentive to others, and the way I acted and reacted to different situations began to shift. Even my family noticed. I no longer aligned with them, and I admit it wasn't easy. Though I wanted to explain what was happening inside me, in a way, they didn't really want to know. I did my best not to be diverted from my path while staying aware that this was my soul's choice and that I needed to honor this great mission.

It was surprising for me to see how easily I was assimilating these new teachings—and I must say, that's still the case today. I began my initiation with the joy of meeting each of the Cosmic Specialists, and I must admit I really enjoyed it. Later on, I had the privilege of working alongside all the Specialists of the physical body. I can assure you that they are numerous, each with their own specific expertise. For example, the Eye Specialist works exclusively on the healing of the eyes.

It was then that I realized I was going to meet many new friends. I also discovered that each had a unique vibration and that there was no hierarchy among them. These beings are disarmingly humble and make sure never to make anyone feel that they are more important. They are fully aware that we evolve in a different density, with a physical body, and that's why they treat us with great respect.

The Cosmic Specialists possess vibrations that are very gentle, subtle, yet incredibly powerful. Over time, it becomes easy to recognize who is present to perform a healing with you. Our role is to ask, and they will gladly carry it out. However, if you ask for something that is not right, nothing will happen.

From one day to the next, I began to apply the teachings of the wonderful Specialists. They would ask, and I would follow through, because I knew deep within that it was the right thing to do. I must admit, many times I warned them they'd better not be "tricking" me, because things wouldn't go well when I got back home. I could hear them laughing! They knew me very well—better than any human who has ever been part of my life, including my family.

I've often heard people say that a single session using the tools is equivalent to several appointments with a healthcare specialist. Because I master the knowledge of the physical body's functioning, in addition to the energetic care, I also explain what the body is trying to communicate. I check with my clients to see if the message I receive for them resonates. The most important thing is that I involve them in their journey back to self-love, and as soon as they reclaim their rightful place, anything becomes possible. Without the conscious involvement of my clients, there wouldn't be all these inexplicable results that many people talk about.

When I think about all the physical memories that the Cosmic Specialists have removed from the holistic bodies of so many individuals, I'm sure no earthly practitioner would ever say to their patient: "Sorry, but your shoulder pain is linked to a dagger lodged in your energetic body. I'll refer you to Isabelle St Germain so she can remove it in a just and perfect way—and the pain will disappear just as it appeared..."

The day this happens, that practitioner will have already taken one of my trainings. I mention this because I've taught several human specialists, and some now openly use this revolutionary method with their patients.

That's also why the entire medical field should have access to this knowledge. More and more countries are beginning to recognize certain energy healing techniques, but we're still far from our goal. Hospitals are filled with people whose problems stem from repressed emotions to the extent that they can no longer breathe with ease. Others are struggling with entities latched onto them, draining their energy, leaving them constantly exhausted. Not to mention those whose physical memory has been triggered in the body, causing such intense pain that they no longer know how to sit or lie down without being "doubled over," praying for it to stop.

And for all the people who are highly empathetic and feel the physical, emotional, and psychological suffering of others—don't you think it would be easier to activate an emotional empathy-releasing spiral than to believe they're simply ill? Naturally, those whose empathy is very strong often end up at a human specialist because they are experiencing all the symptoms of someone else's illness, whether a passerby or a family member.

Have you ever felt perfectly fine in your body, only to walk into a large store and suddenly feel unwell, start coughing, or get a headache? That's the result of empathy. Now you know that if you're highly sensitive to others' pain, you can easily free yourself from it.

Learning to use energetic tools takes practice, and above all, the belief that everything is right and perfect. All you have to do is ask, and the tools activate quickly. The joy of living will always be your greatest, helping you maintain a high vibrational frequency throughout an energetic session.

There are many energetic tools, and it's not necessary to memorize them all. You can use small reference cards to help you relax, as people often fear making mistakes or asking for the wrong thing. What you need to know is that an energetic tool can never harm anyone. If it's not the right tool, it simply won't activate.

I had thousands of hours of experimentation, and I can tell you that I didn't always ask for the right energetic tool. When that happened, I knew the Specialists of Atlantis were standing beside me with their arms crossed and a little smile. They wanted me to understand that it wasn't exactly what the person needed. I would simply try again and continue the session I was conducting.

They often laughed with me, because I didn't memorize all the tools. At the beginning, I would often explain an activation like this: "the thingy that removes implants" or "the little gadget that fixes the information." The goal wasn't for me to overload my memory with all that information, but to gradually understand the logic of the physical body and all those precious energetic tools.

You can't even imagine how many fits of laughter I had during all those experiences. Even though I knew it was serious, such strange phenomena occurred that I couldn't believe they were real. One day, while I was doing an energy treatment for a friend, she told me that she couldn't ground herself to the Earth, feeling as though she was floating. When I focused my awareness on her feet, I saw an image from a past life where she was hanging on a wall, her little feet flailing in all directions. That experience made me laugh. I asked her soul what I needed to do and followed the instructions. When I was done, she was grounded again and the sensation of floating had disappeared.

Is all of this magical? That's what I used to think, but it's actually just logical, not magical. Since you have an aspect or part of yourself that has "run off" to another vibrational plane or parallel reality, you'll feel a void inside and get the sense that you're not fully present within yourself. You'll feel scattered—and that's exactly what's happening.

One day, I was in Paris waiting for a client in a room about twenty square meters in size. As soon as she arrived, she sat in the chair in front of me, and strangely, I could see her standing by the door at the same time. I asked her if she often felt scattered, and she replied that it was the story of her life. The same happens with children who suddenly fall from a tree, or a baby who falls on their bottom and is startled in that moment. These phenomena also occur frequently during accidents. The light bodies separate and don't always realign afterward. The affected person will feel like they're "not living their life" but rather enduring it or watching it go by without being the main actor.

Communication with the Soul

Working consciously with these beings of light is probably the most wonderful discovery I've made. I carried out a lot of tests. Sometimes I asked the same question in different ways to see if the answers would change. The only thing that changed was my soul's response, saying: "You can ask your question in many ways, the answer will always be the same." It's truly amazing to know that our soul knows everything about us and what we've had to experience along our life path. It knows every unimaginable possibility we might experience depending on the choices we make. Nothing is ever set in stone—everything is flexible and malleable.

I needed to understand how my soul was communicating with me, because I couldn't see, feel, or hear anything. I just *knew*. That wasn't enough for me, because I had to share these teachings, and working with the invisible isn't always simple. I felt the need for confirmation, and many times it was difficult to trust this inner knowing that, in truth, seemed so obvious.

So I asked my soul to communicate with me in a different way. From that moment on, my head physically moved side to side or up and down every time I asked a question. It worked—but it wasn't very practical, as it also happened when I was talking with people. Sometimes, my head would sway nonstop, and the worst was when someone lied to me. To confirm, I'd ask the person if they might be exaggerating a little. Often, a small smile would appear on their face, confirming it. That's when I asked my soul to communicate with me more discreetly, and since then, the effect only happens inside my head. Much more comfortable, I must admit!

There are many ways to communicate with your soul, such as through colors, expansion or opening in the heart area, yes or no signals, chills, or inner conversation. It's up to you to discover how your soul and the beings of light choose to connect with you.

You don't need to kneel down to address your soul or a being of light. I suggest always speaking to them the same way you would ask advice from a close friend. By respecting yourself, you'll naturally respect these beautiful light-consciousnesses who are waiting with so much love for these moments when they can assist, guide, or simply answer your questions.

I can tell you that I've asked thousands of questions, and each time, the answer came in the present moment. I even wondered whether one day they'd stop answering because I'd bought into the idea that they'd get tired of my constant questioning. That never happened. As soon as a question is asked, a response comes. But you must ask yourself: Are you really ready to receive the information? Many people say they want guidance, but the fear of being judged runs deep in every human dimension. Often, deep inside, the idea of "worthiness" echoes strongly, and it's easier to say, "I don't receive information or hear anything," than to say, "I believe I don't deserve to receive beautiful and powerful guidance. And if I'm not aligned enough or radiating enough love for myself, will they still answer me?"

From experience, I can confirm the answer always comes. However, I suggest not asking if you aren't ready to hear the response. I know this because I've experienced it myself. When we receive an answer we don't like, it's easy to think we weren't clear enough, weren't in a high enough vibrational state, or that it was just our own mind giving the answer we wanted. Here's my advice: if you ask a question and the answer is no, then don't continue in that direction—you won't like the outcome.

Let me share what happened the last time I didn't listen and went against what I'd been told.

It was December 26th, and I was supposed to visit a friend. I took a moment to ask my soul if it was for my highest good to leave that day. My soul said no. Since it was early morning, I figured I wasn't very aligned. I centered myself, grounded to the Earth, and asked again. The answer didn't change. I decided to go anyway. The whole drive was perfect—nothing to report. When I arrived at my friend's house, I noticed her garage door was open and realized she must have stepped out.

I reversed to park on the side of her house and felt something strange—I thought it was just ice. After a few maneuvers, trying to position my car, I hit the gas and heard a noise. Oops! I had backed into a bright orange marker post used to outline the driveway for snow plowing. It got stuck under my car. As a result, I had to pay $500 for repairs because my rear bumper was damaged.

That was the last time I ignored my soul's guidance. It wasn't the first unpleasant experience, but I sincerely hope it will be the last! All of that just to say: I wanted so badly to go to my friend's that I didn't even need to ask my soul. I didn't *want* to hear the truth.

Remember: it's essential to raise your vibrational frequency to ensure you receive clear answers from your soul.

If you want to experience this new concept, go immediately to page 150, Exercise #12

Enjoy your discovery! Raising the Vibrational Frequency

As I've been telling you since the beginning of your reading, I truly wish that, while going through this book, you pay attention to the cells within you that contain the knowledge of Atlantis. Doing so would allow you to awaken those that lie dormant inside you. You have every right to ask your soul at any moment for this to unfold gently. And so it shall be.

I can already hear you asking: "How do we ask for this?"

Know that the process is very simple and easy.

Here's how to do it:

"I address my entire holistic body. I ask you to awaken all this knowledge that lies dormant within me and to bring it back to my conscious awareness gently and in respect of who I am, here and now. Thank you!"

The more you speak to your holistic body, the more readily the information will be revealed to you. Pretty great, isn't it? I simply ask you to do this regularly and let go. You never know what might be placed before your eyes that will trigger these openings of consciousness. However, I suggest you don't ask for this if you're not willing to see and relive scenes from a past incarnation of your soul that may have lived in Atlantis.

It's important to remember that this approach is not meant as a test. You cannot ask and then withdraw because you realize the results are actually happening.

Be in harmony with your heart and start by asking whether it's for your highest good—just like you did before beginning the reading of this book. Now turn your attention inward. If you feel an expansion or some form of opening, then the answer is positive. I suggest you practice to better understand what a "yes" and a "no" feel like from your soul.

The best way to find out is to ask short and direct questions.

Here are a few examples to guide you:

- "I address my soul: Am I a woman?"
- "I address my soul: Am I a crocodile?"
- "I address my soul: Is my birthday in November?"
- "I address my soul: Do I have 5 minor-aged children?"
- "I address my soul: Are my eyes green?"
- "I address my soul: Do I own a house in the countryside?"

I encourage you to make your own list of questions—and of course, make sure your vibrational frequency is very high before doing these exercises so that your answers are precise.

If you'd rather address a guide, an archangel, or your heart, don't hesitate to do so. The answers will come to you just the same. The more you practice, the more you'll enjoy developing your communication with the invisible.

The Law of Return and the Sacred Tools

Whenever I traveled to Atlantis to understand how the physical body functions or to explore various devices, my consciousness was always directed toward what I needed in the present moment. As soon as I received the teaching or information, I had to return to my here and now. Sometimes, this was frustrating because I had glimpsed new energetic tools, and since I'm naturally very curious, I would have loved to know what they were for. But I can tell you—it doesn't work that way. You can't just be there for the sake of being there; you must have a good reason. There's no room for wandering. So, if you're setting out to discover Atlantis, make sure it's for a good reason—otherwise, you won't be allowed to enter the island.

There were times when I wasn't allowed to experiment because my vibrational frequency didn't allow it. I knew I could always return at a more favorable time. The moment our thoughts start scattering and we lose focus, our vibrational frequency drops quickly.

During one of my authorized journeys, I discovered that in a past incarnation, when my soul lived in Atlantis, it had developed a remote control with three keyboards. On one of my visits to the island, I was taken into a room where there were several computers with very large bluish screens. One of the guides who was accompanying me

(because I'm never left alone) explained to me how the remote worked. A screen was on the top part, and once it was turned on, I could bring up the image of a person or part of the physical body using my thoughts, and depending on the buttons I pressed, I could see the entire dysfunction.

The remote was used to reprogram, harmonize, dissolve, realign, and release. I had three keyboards full of different functions to bring the physical body back to its original state of health. I found it very interesting. When I asked if I could use it in my healing sessions, the guide looked at me and indicated that I first needed to learn how the physical body works.

One day, I asked the being accompanying me if they would kindly bring me the remote. Physically, I felt the remote settle into my hand. Of course, the object was energetic.

In the days that followed, I was so happy to be able to share this new technology. From that moment on, there was almost always someone trying to claim it. That wasn't very cool, so I returned it to Atlantis to keep it safe. This experience helped me understand what the guide meant when he told me to start by learning the body's functions before using the remote. He wasn't joking—and I can confirm that they never joke in Atlantis.

In other words, I had chosen not to take the guide's words seriously, and I received the return that came with not respecting the instruction given.

Remember the law of cause and effect mentioned earlier in this book.

Chapter 2: My Apprenticeship

Throughout my apprenticeship, I became aware of the perfect and rightful order of things. The physical body is very complex, and I discovered that when one part of the body is ill, in a way, the entire body is also unwell.

I spent hundreds of hours experimenting, understanding, and most importantly, remembering the functionalities of the brain. These are extremely complex, and since they govern the entire holistic body, it was important for me to take everything into account. I realized that I didn't need to know everything about human anatomy and physiology to succeed. I only needed to have an overall understanding, fortunately, because it's truly very complicated.

There is also a grid structure surrounding each part of the anatomy. It is represented by a checkered sphere, and when a part of the body is sick, its grid is affected. Often, we will see small segments that are darker or missing. We must therefore consider many factors before reaching vibrational reconstruction.

The physical body also includes several bodies of light that surround it like Russian nesting dolls. Among these bodies of light is the alphanumeric body. Within it are inscribed the source codes for each anatomical part. A source code contains several numbers, and when a part of the body is sick, the numbers turn off one by one. We must therefore ensure to reset the source codes. As a small clarification, everything I write here regarding energetic knowledge is based on the Atlanteans' learning during their medical studies. For them, the physical and the energetic were inseparable.

You must now fully understand that before diving into energetic healing, it's important to know what you are doing. We must act consciously and ask ourselves what is right and good to do before taking action, rather than reflecting only afterward. One cannot simply declare oneself a master of this or that after attending a few days of training. That's a bit absurd, as there is so much to remember, understand, and experiment with on oneself before developing the necessary skills to offer healing to others.

Always be very vigilant to avoid falling into the trap that may arise from thinking you're better than others. You will always be the most important person that exists on Earth—but only in your own life. This, of course, applies to every other human being as well. Taking a step back will always be appropriate throughout your journey of expanding consciousness.

What I understood during my apprenticeship with the Atlanteans is that everything that exists on the physical level also exists on the energetic level. The only difference is that on the energetic level, there are no side effects, and you cannot receive too much either. The body is of such extreme intelligence. When we perform an exercise repeatedly, the releases occur layer by layer. Remember that as long as the initial source has not been recognized, accepted and released, the energetic tools will continue to work again and again. However, when there is nothing left to release on a given subject, the tools will simply stop activating.

The funniest part is seeing the Specialists right next to us, waiting to see what we're going to do, understand, and especially what to ask them for. They are always ready and available for us, 24/7.

To be able to work with all these sacred tools, I had to go through many experiences that were neither pleasant nor easy to understand from the perspective of a "standard" human being. However, it is precisely because of those experiences that I can now transmit these precious teachings with absolute confidence.

When I first started using the tools, part of me knew exactly what it was doing, while another part questioned whether I might be a little unbalanced in the head. Nevertheless, I followed the guidance. Day after day, new energetic tools came into my awareness, and I used them without a single doubt.

Each time, this new little wonder was perfectly suited to the person receiving the energy treatment. It brought me joy and a quiet pride. I didn't show it much, because my biggest fear was ending up "on a cloud," believing I was better than others. For years, I asked my guides to make sure I stayed grounded. The answer was always the same: "Don't worry, that won't happen." It was reassuring, and yet a part of me remained very vigilant.

What I find rather amusing is that whenever I perform a healing session and a new energetic tool presents itself to me, I instantly know what it does and what it's called. They all have names. However, not all of them are words found in our dictionary. I must keep the given name intact because each tool holds a unique and powerful vibration.

In the beginning, when I was just starting to perform energy healing and receive various sacred tools—whether for removing an implant, a physical memory, an emotional burden, or even traces of magic or sorcery—I knew exactly what to ask for. As soon as I was done, people would say things like: "It's incredible, I feel no more pain," or "I can move my arm again," or "I feel really light inside." For me, it was done without any doubt, as if I had been doing this my whole life. Over time, I received more and more treasures. Eventually, I began teaching these techniques that I found so captivating.

I've experimented a lot, and to this day, I'm still just as fascinated whenever I discover something new. I must admit that it's thrilling—but it also means going through even more rounds of energetic clearing and healing. That part isn't always enjoyable. It's never physically painful, but emotionally, it can be tiring to constantly be revisiting and releasing. It's not that the tools don't work—it's just that with each new "veil" lifted, there are still old memories, imprints, and traces to be cleared.

At one point, I even asked my guides why they didn't show me everything right from the start. It would have been so much easier—or so I thought. But they told me that if they had, I would never have developed the perseverance I now have. I accept that and acknowledge it. Still, if I compare the tools I received at the beginning with those I receive now, they're quite different. That said, I still use the original foundational tools I received more than twenty years ago, and they are just as precious today. What I would have truly appreciated, however, is a complete course on the constitution of the holistic body from the start. As you can probably guess, patience is not my strongest quality, though I've made a lot of progress over the years.

The only time my patience is limitless is when I'm teaching or doing an energy session. I can explain things in many different ways, for as long as it takes for someone to understand. I don't pretend to know someone else's truth, but the information I receive is accurate. I simply pass it along with as much simplicity as possible. My only task is to find the right way to communicate it without hurting the person while still delivering the messages I receive.

Through my visits to Atlantis, I discovered that everything I know and everything I do during a healing session, a past incarnation of my soul had already studied and mastered. That incarnation had a deep passion to explore the workings of the human body. Alongside other researchers and scientists, we managed to dissect the different dimensions of every anatomical part—physically, mentally, emotionally, spiritually, and in the realm of infinite love consciousness. By the way, concerning the dimension of infinite love consciousness, I've never discovered a single dysfunction, disqualified energy, implant, or physical memory at that level. That's truly exceptional!

I honed my experience by spending countless hours exploring the energetic dimensions of the holistic body, performing clearings, repairs, and even energetic surgeries. What continues to fascinate me is that all of these experiences happen completely naturally, as if it's second nature. I've discovered that in the present moment, I always know exactly what to do, how to do it, and which energetic tools to use.

Hundreds of people have crossed my path and received teachings about energetic tools. I have written and delivered more than 19 different training programs. I know that these individuals have all experienced significantly greater results in their practice because they used these sacred tools. At least, those who dared to use them, as all these tools require us to use our voice and ask in order to receive. Even in 2025, many of them have not dared to make that choice for fear of judgment. Everything is perfect because these individuals know that the day they wish to, the tools will always be available.

I would love to be present to see your first experiences. It's always very amusing to see the expressions on people's faces because almost everyone reacts the same way. They look around to make sure they're alone. They take deep breaths. They begin by asking for permission and from that very moment, their voice changes, worry rises within them, and they begin to feel hot. Often, they put it off, telling themselves that all of this must be nonsense. Days go by, and a little voice brings them back to that simple little procedure that's very easy to perform.

You must know that no matter what you wish to learn, as long as you don't experiment, you will never know whether or not you truly have that incredible creative power within you. Choose to make experience your best friend, and the more joy you bring to it, the more amazed you will be by the results.

I suggest you use your voice instead of whispering. Speak with determination and you will quickly learn to move energy intensely. You can speak in your head, and for some people this works very well. However, make sure you are fully focused on what you are doing, because if your mind is elsewhere, the energy will be scattered and it won't have the same positive impact.

Start with small exercises and then gradually add elements. For those who believe they don't have any free time to take care of themselves, I suggest experimenting while you're doing your personal hygiene. Stand in front of the mirror and while brushing your teeth, start by looking yourself in the eyes. Offer yourself a beautiful smile. By paying attention to your eyes, you'll see that they shine brighter and are very sensitive to everything you say. Sometimes, you might feel like they're getting bigger, and over time, you'll discover that it's not just a feeling—it's really happening.

The more you speak to your physical body with kindness and gentleness, the more your facial features will respond quickly. Once you realize that everything is recorded in your eyes, you will begin to look at them differently. They are filled with energetic veils that contain all the memories of what you have seen and what has marked you. You must now understand that it's no coincidence if vision deteriorates over time.

What's less pleasant for me is that my body reacts to everything, and immediately. I cannot say or even think something without having a direct reaction if I'm not aligned with the recognition, pride, and appreciation of my entire being. You can imagine that it's not always very funny, because I talk a lot. Even when I'm teaching and I use words or expressions to explain the law of cause and effect, my body doesn't distinguish. So, I need to do a lot of releases and speak to my earthly transport vehicle very often, if I want it to stay aligned. Sometimes, I simply forget, and it takes me a while to understand what it reacted to. You can't lie to your holistic body, so you must understand that the fewer words you use—and the more absolutely accurate they are—the more beautiful your energy will be. Your physical body will be very happy.

As soon as an emotion rises within you, it will intensify the return of what you've just said or thought. I suggest learning to laugh internally and to make joy vibrate—then you'll see that the return will be much more pleasant. It's not easy, but the goal is to reclaim your creative power. The more aware you become of the words you use, the more your physical body will maintain its holistic health. This means in all its emotional, physical, psychological and energetic components.

Learning to reclaim one's personal power of self-love, understanding how the holistic body functions, and daring to have your own experiences will remain, for me, the greatest adventure. Don't assume that everything works on the first try every time, because that wouldn't be true. Sometimes, what I ask for doesn't hold up, so I have to rethink what I said and reformulate it properly. That's the main reason I advocate speaking out loud. This way, you can hear yourself. Always be precise, and I suggest getting straight to the point so you don't get lost in your requests.

It's also important to note that, most of the time, those who choose to return to themselves on a journey of awakening tend to think it's a good idea to place protective layers around themselves. Twenty years ago, that was truly ideal.

Today, it is imperative to understand that all those protections lead to confinement—even imprisonment. So, it's important to remember that love for yourself will always be your greatest protection.

This vibration of love is not an emotion but a state of the soul that must resonate from your heart and emanate through all dimensions of your holistic Being.

When I began practicing energy healing with energetic tools, I sensed that I was familiar with this science, but I didn't understand how I had learned it, since I had studied various subjects in this present life but not that one. When I inquired about how an energetic tool manifests, the Atlantean Guides explained that it is essential to grasp the vibration of life in all things. I can confirm that my ears were wide open because I was genuinely curious about what they were going to share with me.

Here is what they explained: the vibration of life in all things is the same vibration that is part of the greater Whole. It has characteristics that make up everything that exists. When we manifest a tool, we associate this vibration with the original frequency of a system, an organ, a blood cell, or a molecule, depending on the healing need.

Then we gather the energy of the universal manifestation plane and fuse it with this vibration.

These tools were manifested over a long period because the problems are similar at their core but different overall. Many experiments were conducted before the tool that perfectly matched the need was sealed and protected.

Depending on the person's level of surrender, the tools will respond more or less quickly. The soul state, vibrational frequency of the person being treated, and the place where they are located will have a direct impact. This is the main reason for my warning. I remind you again to always make sure you are working within a very high vibrational frequency and that joy is present during the treatment.

Over time, I understood that by combining energetic tools and communication with my physical body, the results were always very surprising and significant. Since I've almost always wanted to understand things, I asked so many questions, and sometimes the answers didn't satisfy me, so I asked my questions differently. You can't even imagine how many times I rephrased my questions, and one day, my soul replied: "You can ask the same question in different ways as many times as you want—the answer will always be the same." I believe I needed to hear that response for faith to become absolute within me.

So, from the moment everything aligned perfectly with the truth of my heart, I knew that what I was receiving was right, and I could pass on the information.

If you wish to experiment with this new concept,
turn immediately to page 150, Exercise #13.

Enjoy the discovery! Understanding and Honoring the Truth of Your Heart.

Chapter 3: Energy Healings and the Sacred Tools of Atlantis

At the same time that I began to channel and receive numerous pieces of information from my guides, I also started receiving knowledge about sacred energetic tools. Here is the teaching I received at the very beginning when I experienced this shift at the soul level. My guides told me the following:

"From now on, it will be important that all the energetic interventions you perform are done within a very high vibrational frequency to ensure that the interventions are correct and perfect. Always invite the Archangelic plane to be present with you, ask for the vibrational frequency of your entire holistic being, your place of residence, as well as the person and their place of residence, to be elevated. Also ask for the opening of a great wells of light above you, your place of residence, and for the person and their place of residence, so that everything that is disqualified may return to the light. It is important to remember that it is inappropriate to send everything back to the Earth, because it causes storms, hurricanes, and volcanic eruptions."

When you think about it, it's true that the Earth holds a great amount of water, which symbolizes emotion. If we transmit all our anger, hatred, jealousy, envy, and so on to her, it's obvious that one day, Gaia will expel it.

The Roots of Light and Platforms

From the very beginning, I understood that regardless of the client in front of me, I had to start my session by grounding them to the Earth. All human beings possess roots of light. There are human, divine, masculine, and feminine roots that I considered during my consultations. I had to examine their energetic structure because often there were flaws, and sometimes their roots were nearly nonexistent. Those with the weakest grounding almost always shared a common point: their relationship with their mother, whether it was their own mother, the mother within, or the mother who raised or abandoned them.

The least pleasant experience for these people is that, eventually, their roots will become nearly nonexistent. It is through grounding to the Earth that we nourish the joints of the holistic body. The expected outcomes are arthritis, osteoarthritis, and fibromyalgia. These are all very painful and difficult symptoms to endure.

In order for the healing results to be conclusive, it was imperative for me to bring my clients to the awareness that they needed to accept and acknowledge everything that had occurred in their mother-child relationship.

Sometimes, I would see platforms running through the roots horizontally or diagonally. The initial source of these platforms was connected to some form of dependency. Depending on the person I was treating, I would sometimes discover that the platforms belonged to their genealogy. It was wild to see bottles of alcohol or a little mountain of chocolate in the energy. I always took the time to confirm with them whether what I was seeing was true in their life or not. I can confirm that, very often, people would smile in positive confirmation!

Did you know that a child who was not loved, welcomed, acknowledged, and treated as the greatest treasure by his or her mother while young, will eventually convince themselves that if their own mother did not love them, then they do not deserve to be loved by Gaia, Mother Earth? As a result, they will struggle to find their place on Earth and will not easily ground themselves either. Therefore, I had to find a way to make my clients aware of this process so that I could deeply anchor their roots of light and make them strong, vibrant, and luminous.

To achieve this, I would simply ask for the pure crystal waterfall of Atlantis to pour down over all the roots to completely dissolve them. Then, I would ask Gaia to regenerate new ones. Following this intervention, people often felt as if their feet were sinking into the floor and becoming very heavy. It was important to me that this happened in this way because it validated my work and made it tangible in the material world for them.

The Unspoken Words

Afterwards, I took the time to observe the unspoken. You know, everything you don't dare to say for fear of being rejected, abandoned, ignored, and so on. Know that all these unspoken words settle in your sacred speech channel, and all the emotional charge they carry becomes compacted in your jaw. Since my main working tool is my voice, I learned to ask aloud and thus receive everything I needed to give these energy healings. It was also important for the person to hear the procedure to avoid any unpleasant surprises.

What was less pleasant for me was the empathy. Very often, I would start coughing because it was really heavy at that level, and I could feel it in my throat. So I would quickly release those unspoken words by activating the interstellar ejector spirals. They were specially designed to perform these releases. Sometimes, I had to ask them to activate at power 3 or 4. It was even more powerful but still very gentle at the same time for humans.

I quickly remembered that when we release something, we often recover cellular memories, imprints, traces, shadows, etc. I therefore had to make sure that everything that was disqualified would return to the light. It was by pouring the turquoise, scarlet, violet, orange, silver, pastel, gold, and diamond balms that everything was completely released. Since the body was marked, and to activate the process of cellular and molecular regeneration, I had to pour the golden, pink, and violet flame balms after each release.

You can imagine that it was a lot to remember, but day by day, the information returned to my memory and it became natural for me to use it in every energy session. There were no limitations or restrictions.

However, logic always had to be present. I didn't study the science of the physical body in this life, but when I performed a healing, my conscious memory would instantly reactivate the knowledge I needed. I asked many questions in the energy field because too often, clients hesitated to tell me the real reason they came to see me. I can understand that a person who has been abused, beaten, or raped may not find it easy to discuss those topics. Yet, I received the information and it was up to me to find the appropriate way to communicate with my client. The energy of fear, shame and disgust still vibrated within these individuals, along with guilt, which occupied a large emotional space within them.

I couldn't withhold the transmission of these valuable pieces of information I was receiving. Since emotional burden is the root of many pathologies, if people truly want to heal, it is important for me to speak openly and authentically with them. Powerful releases may follow from this new understanding.

Do not believe for a moment that my visions were always 100% accurate, nor that people would say, "That's exactly what I experienced with my father, or my partner, or my mother, or an uncle." That is not the truth. Nevertheless, they often nodded or responded with their eyes.

Afterwards, to enable the release, I used the emotional ejector spirals, specifying the source to transmute, such as anger, anxiety, shame, guilt, regret and so on. I asked them to accept and recognize that all the time spent recalling difficult past experiences only compressed those emotions more and more inside them. I encouraged them to breathe deeply and to completely let go of those emotions.

This intervention didn't change their past stories, but it allowed them to stop feeling or feeding those painful memories. It could take several sessions for those living in denial. It often takes longer because they don't want to recall certain painful events, and that's perfectly natural.

Did you know that the physical body is designed in such a way that before feeling discomfort, injury, or illness, the impact is first lodged in the light bodies? It's only when these become saturated that they settle in the physical body. This brings us back to the idea that we would do well to take care of our light bodies and perform emotional releases as often as possible. It will take about one minute of your earthly time. The longest part is simply asking, because everything happens in that very instant.

Physical Memories

The Specialists introduced me to "physical memories" almost at the very beginning. You can easily imagine that I had no idea what that could possibly mean. Here is what they explained to me.

A physical memory represents a way in which a past incarnation died. If someone was killed by a spear, dagger, arrow, bomb, or blade to the back, and this caused their death, then in this current life, that memory can reactivate. For example, if this person experiences several betrayals, one of these memories may awaken, and the pain will be as intense as if it were physically happening. As long as it remains present in the energy field, the pain will persist.

I began receiving clients with phantom pain in their shoulder blades. Some could no longer lift their arms very high because the pain was too intense. Upon questioning them, I quickly realized that they had all experienced betrayal on multiple occasions. At first, it took a very long time to release physical memories because I had to proceed step by step, using laser rays, oils, and balms. I also had to create a space where the memory was located to remove any dried blood or metal residue, depending on the signs that emerged.

It wasn't very fun because it really took a lot of time. I experimented with releasing these memories in this way for several years before learning how to remove them in just a few seconds. What I found most astonishing was that my clients no longer experienced pain after the session. Everything had disappeared, as if by magic.

There are many physical memories. The most common ones are:

- the slavery harness on the shoulders

- balls and chains on the ankles
- wooden legs
- helmets on the head
- of course, arrows in the back
- arms and hands that had been cut off
- everything I previously mentioned around the shoulder blades

Honestly, nothing surprises me anymore. So, if you are experiencing pain in your shoulder blades, the question to ask yourself is: *"Is there a physical memory active within me?"*

Here's the story of my first physical memory release. A woman came to see me for an energy healing session. She was convinced that I wouldn't believe what she was feeling. According to her, there was a large hole in the middle of her stomach and she could even feel air passing through it. I listened attentively to what she was telling me, and suddenly, I saw a scene from a war. A person had died from a cannonball wound to the abdomen. I tend to laugh when I see these scenes, because at first glance, it seems like pure imagination, doesn't it?

I immediately shared my vision with her. I used my energy tools to remove the physical memory from her belly and, with the help of different balms, I closed the hole in her abdomen. Instantly, the sensation disappeared and never returned. This woman was so happy to no longer feel the wind passing through her. Luckily, I had my energy tools!

A Chamber of Time's Incompressibility, Time Corridors, and Space-Time

It is important to always take into account the emotional charge that has been locked away, repressed, denied, or sometimes buried. There would never be dysfunction in health if destructive emotions didn't exist. For example, guilt, rejection, abandonment, bitterness, and the most destructive of all—death. It is essential to always release the emotional energy from the past if you wish to achieve good results.

And that's not all. You see, when we look with our physical eyes, we simply see a body. However, when knowledge awakens within us, multiple dimensions and vibratory planes open up, offering a wealth of information about everything that has been experienced through speech, thought, events, situations, emotions, and the people involved.

For example, when you have a problem with your eyes, you must first examine the vision you hold of yourself to assess the destructive impact this will have on your near vision. On the other hand, fear of the future, such as fear of aging, being alone, becoming a burden to your loved ones, lacking money, or losing your independence, will negatively impact your distance vision. All of this information is recorded in various vibrational or energetic planes and dimensions, if you prefer.

By opening these spaces, you will also recover all the images that have marked you, everything you never want to see again, all the looks that were cast upon you (including those from your parents or partners), and those you cast upon others. Everything you have seen in this current life is indeed recorded.

In addition to all these vibrational planes and dimensions, there also exist a chamber of time's incompressibility. When one of these is opened, the entire history of the eye, for example, is recorded there. There is one for everything that exists. You can understand that a single session of energy healing cannot lead to the complete release of everything that causes dysfunction in a part of the physical body.

Thus, if I open the chamber of time's incompressibility, I will discover everything you have lived, said, done, thought, etc., from the very first second of your conception until now. A time corridor holds all the experiences related to a specific subject. For instance, by opening the time corridor of anger, I will see all the people involved and every situation you experienced when you generated that emotion. A space-time is a little harder to explain. In fact, it is a space created between time corridors. You can find a variety of experiences there, connected to the surrounding corridors.

I must explain all these details to you because, when performing energy healing on someone, if we lack this knowledge, many sessions will be necessary before reaching the root cause of the issue. It's also important to understand that when everything opens across the 22 vibrational planes and dimensions, it resembles a multitude of highways intersecting in all directions. The same energy linked to an emotion can manifest everywhere simultaneously or only in specific places.

Ejecting Spirals

When I began performing energy healing, I learned to use the powerful spirals that Atlantean children had created. Each one had a different function. I quickly realized that whenever I requested the activation of one of these spirals, it always started from the center of the Earth, passed through the roots of light, and then through the entire holistic body (the physical body, energy centers, and the light bodies).

These light bodies surround the physical body, nested like Russian dolls. I was surprised when people began asking me if it was normal to feel something spinning inside them, sometimes like a top. Through feedback from my clients, I quickly learned to trust my energy tools.

I truly enjoyed discovering all these treasures. However, there was a time when I asked the Specialists to slow down a bit. I felt there were too many different elements to memorize, and they laughed a lot again. It was their friendly way of helping me understand that I needed to stop putting so much pressure on myself. They revealed to me that, over time, this knowledge would naturally settle within me because it was already part of my soul's acquisitions. Everything would return to my conscious awareness at the right moment.

And indeed, that's exactly what happened.

Personal and Others' Emotional Ejecting Spiral

When I perform an energy healing session for someone, I must release all the emotional buildup that has been accumulated and is trapped in the various parts of the body, as well as across different levels and vibrational planes.

It was therefore important for me to have a tool to enable this release. I learned to use the *personal and others' emotional ejecting spiral*. It activates from the heart of Gaia, Mother Earth. It travels through all the roots of light and rises through the entirety of the holistic body.

I quickly understood that I needed to remind my clients to breathe during their activation because I could often feel the energy getting blocked in the throat.

Sometimes, we experience the emotions of others just as intensely as if they were our own. This is why the spiral works on both personal and others' emotional energy.

The more precise I am in my requests, the more powerful the releases are. I used to say that you shouldn't make a vegetable soup and mix everything together, because the results won't be as significant.

Imagine one day, during a visit to your doctor, they openly talk to you about the emotional charge of anger compressed behind your stomach, which is causing a burning sensation in your abdomen.

Now imagine they ask you to accept and acknowledge that you are still angry with your father, who humiliated you in front of the entire family when you were a child. They then offer to activate a beautiful *personal and others' emotional ejecting spiral* to release this anger, suggesting that you become aware that you cannot change what happened in the past. They teach you that it's possible to address your father either energetically or in person and simply say:

"I address you, Dad. I realize now that since you humiliated me in front of the family during a Christmas dinner, I've harbored a lot of anger toward you. I now understand that this anger no longer has any purpose or place in my holistic body. It's time I free myself from the past. Thank you, Dad, for the experience."

After saying these words, your doctor suggests you breathe out of love for yourself and for your liberation from the past. Would you listen? Would you be willing to give it a try?

Emotions clutter many dimensions of the holistic body. By realizing that you are using your vital energy to create destructive emotions, you will quickly recognize that it's true that everything begins with yourself. The law of return is indeed at work.

If you wish to explore this new concept, go directly to page 152, exercise #14.

Enjoy the discovery! Releasing Memories of the Past.

Interstellar Ejecting Spiral

Did you know that unspoken words often lead to colds, flus, and can even worsen into bronchitis or pneumonia? The right tool for releasing these unspoken words is the *interstellar ejecting spiral*. It activates in the same way as the others—from the heart of Gaia.

As long as the same emotion continues to be generated, the spiral will need to be used regularly. It's not always easy to avoid feeding fear, doubt, or guilt. This is part of our earthly learning journey. Every part of the physical body holds a very specific emotional charge. Throughout this book, I help you become aware of these associations and invite you to validate for yourself whether they resonate with you or not.

Ejecting Spiral for Miasmas and Astral Debris

There are also miasmas and astral debris often found in the light bodies. If they're never cleared, this debris and miasmas will eventually settle in the physical body, complicating healing. Miasmas attach themselves to you when your astral body travels at night through low-vibration dimensions, or during the day when someone is feeling very unwell and their vibrational frequency drops too low. This leaves the door open for these highly disqualified energies to cling to the holistic body.

There is a *miasma and astral debris ejecting spiral* that can be activated daily to maintain your holistic being. This phenomenon is also found in people who abuse drugs or alcohol. Let me reassure you—it's not because someone has a single glass of wine that they'll end up in these vibrational spaces or planes.

It's also important to know that if your light bodies become saturated, the overflow will settle in your physical body. Therefore, if you're sick and have a wound, it's very likely that the healing and scarring process will take longer. You've understood correctly: the *miasmas and astral debris ejecting spiral* brings significant well-being.

Anecdote

Here's a story I experienced with a friend who came to my house to let me try his pendulum. For my part, I'm not allowed to use any external objects with the sacred tools. However, my friend Gaétan wanted to see if I had any cracks or dysfunctions in my light bodies.

He took his little pendant in hand, intending to use it on me. I immediately said, "Stop. How long has it been since you cleaned your pendulum?" He replied that he never cleaned it. I was very surprised, but I asked him to give it to me.

At that point, I decided to open a pillar of light and perform the cleaning procedure on his pendulum. The operation took me less than a minute. Within 30 seconds, I energetically received all the contents of his pendulum pouring onto my head. It felt like a bucket of eggs had been dumped over me—I could feel the sticky texture sliding down my face.

At that moment, I heard one of my guides laughing, and he simply said: "You must not give the fish. Teach others how to fish." In other words, I should have taught my friend how to clean his pendulum instead of doing it for him.

Moreover, I hadn't asked whether I was authorized to do it. If I had, the answer would have been NO. It's so simple to ask before doing something, rather than facing an unpleasant return. Remember: *getting authorization is the very first step before performing any energy work.*

I learned the lesson well, and since then, I share as much information as possible and ask for permission before doing anything 98% of the time. After that brief conversation with my guide, I used the *miasmas and astral debris ejecting spirals* to cleanse myself from the return. What's really wonderful about sacred tools is that all interventions are done in just a few seconds. In fact, making the request takes longer than the actual release!

I also suggest using this lovely spiral in your homes, especially in places where there's moisture, like basements—because where there is dampness, there are miasmas, and the smell is not very pleasant for the nose.

Emotional, Physical, Psychic, and Psychological Empathy Ejecting Spiral

I'd also like to refresh your memory regarding empathy. As you already know, this term is often misused as if it were synonymous with compassion. However, empathy is something entirely different. Its function is to make you feel the physical, emotional, or psychological pain of others within your own physical body. It was a tool developed by sorcerers and witches in order to help others without ending up burned at the stake.

From now on, when you talk about empathy, be cautious—because the more you claim to be an empathic person, the higher the risk you'll actually feel others' pain.

Rest assured, a true marvel exists to help you free yourself from this. It is called the emotional, physical, psychic, and psychological empathy ejecting spiral. I strongly recommend activating it every day if you have this ability, because you could easily believe you're sick. In fact, it's good to know that it's entirely possible to feel all the symptoms of a particular illness in your own body, when in reality, you're simply sensing what's happening in someone else's physical body whom you may have crossed paths with.

All these tools have no contraindications! You can use them every day, and I strongly suggest that you do. If you think about it, you experience emotions constantly; you interact with people in person, by phone, or through video calls. Your quality of life will improve quickly if you make that choice.

Today on Earth, many people are empathic, and it's not pleasant to go to a restaurant or a market and suddenly feel pain in your arm or stomach when everything was fine before you entered. The only people who manage to free themselves from this entirely and quickly are those who use energetic tools.

Here's the best tip that the guides taught me to determine whether I should activate the empathy ejecting spirals to free myself easily. I just had to ask my soul the following question:

"Dear soul, does what I'm currently feeling in my physical body belong to me or not?"

Whenever I was outside the house and suddenly felt pain or discomfort, I'd ask this question to my soul. When the answer revealed that the pain did not belong to me, I'd joyfully release the sensation by activating the empathy spiral.

Remember, everything is logical—so if I'm in physical pain, it's only natural to be in emotional pain too, because it's rare to be injured without feeling emotion. It's also possible to meet someone with suicidal thoughts and, through empathy, develop suicidal thoughts yourself in the hours following that encounter.

Have you ever had experiences like that? Some people fall into a depressive state and end up taking very strong medication in such cases.

If you wish to explore this new concept, turn to page 153, exercise #15.

Enjoy the discovery! Release of Emotional, Physical, and Psychological Empathy.

Balls of Light

One of the most precious energetic tools I have received is the violet energy ball. It allows me to transform the images, people, and messages I receive from other vibrational planes. I quickly realized I needed to utilize this on everything that presented itself to me, because behind one image, there is often another very different one. Gradually, I noticed that the hidden truth behind appearances was always revealed to me thanks to these violet energy balls. As soon as I saw something in the energy, I would throw these precious balls until everything stopped transforming. This allowed me to swiftly get to the real source of things. Sometimes it was a being of light I was seeing, and when I threw balls at it, it transformed into a rather dark energy. What an extraordinary tool!

I also threw these balls of light at living people, and I quickly realized that those individuals could no longer lie. It was quite funny because they became very uncomfortable; they didn't know what was happening to them. So I got into the habit of throwing violet energy balls at everything that appeared to me.

I invite you to put this into practice, and you'll discover just how powerful and useful this tool is. You may sometimes be disappointed to realize that you've been accompanied for a long time by beings who are neither the master nor the light being you expected. Just know that it's better to realize this later than never.

I understand that many of you might hesitate to try it out because you're afraid of finding out that you've been misled. However, when you're ready, remember that this valuable tool is just waiting for you.

There are also crystal energy balls. These should be used in very small quantities. They are helpful for dissolving cages, prisons, false floors, seals, and symbols, but I suggest clearly specifying that you wish to throw tiny crystal balls.

To soften situations, you can throw pearlescent energy balls. I invite you never to throw them at people.

It is always crucial to remember that in the realm of energy, there are certain rules to follow if you want to obtain good results and most importantly, to avoid receiving a backlash due to the law of cause and effect.

As I mentioned earlier, the first thing to remember is to always ask for permission to perform an energy treatment directly from the person. The people around you may not all be open-minded and may refuse to receive it. If you proceed without their permission, you won't appreciate what happens within and around you in the following days. This act is called interference in someone's light bodies, which means you would be manipulating someone without their knowledge. On Earth, as you know, the law of cause and effect is always in effect. A person who interferes with your light bodies is comparable to committing an energetic violation.

The Crystal of the Source Code of Unity

Within each person, we find distinct parts: the fetus, the baby, the child, the adolescent, the man or woman, the mother or father, the grandmother or grandfather. We also distinguish aspects such as jealousy, envy, anger, victimhood, laziness, authoritarianism, strictness, manipulation, control, denial, as well as multidimensionality, the primitive personality, and the secondary personality.

To achieve lasting results, it is important to take into account the entirety of the holistic being. The tool that was designed to gather all these parts is the Crystal of the Source Code of Unity. As soon as a person is placed within this crystal, we gain access to all the aspects mentioned above.

It's always very interesting to see people's reactions when they realize that each of these parts is present within them. For example, it is essential to understand that even if you are not naturally jealous, jealousy is still a part of you. The same applies to all other aspects of yourself.

I'd like to draw your attention to the fact that everything that happened during your pregnancy is imprinted in the cellular memories of each part of your being. However, it's very different for someone who, for example, was abused during adolescence. The cellular impact of that event will only be found in the man or woman, the mother or father, the grandmother or grandfather. The fetus, baby, and child will thus be spared. This is why it is important to use the crystal before proceeding with a release. It allows you to obtain rapid and extraordinary results on all levels.

Vibrational Frequency

The second essential point to remember concerns vibrational frequency. It must remain very high at all times when you are giving or receiving an energy treatment. The higher the frequency, the more quickly information, releases, and understandings will occur. The lower the vibrational frequency, the more people tend to fall asleep. Why? Because the vibration of the Cosmic Specialists who assist you during treatments is very high, creating a significant vibrational gap when your frequency is too low. That is why it is essential to know the appropriate energetic tools to perform the treatments.

Wells of Light

Let us now speak of the wells of light, the third most important point for you to remember. A well of light is a space that opens within various dimensions and vibrational planes, allowing all that is disqualified to return to the light or be transformed before reintegrating into the physical body. Inside these wells are multiple light cylinders of different colors that facilitate transformation, calibration, or definitive release.

For years, practitioners would send everything disqualified during energy treatments back into the Earth. The proper and essential way to proceed during your energy harmonizations is to request the Angel of Fire to open large wells of light above you, your client, your living space, and theirs (if you are offering remote harmonization). At the end of the session, it is essential to ask that the wells of light be closed.

The being of light who opens these wells is the Angel of Fire—it is part of their role.

When I emphasize the importance of closing the wells of light, it is a precious piece of advice I'm offering. If you do not do so, one day everything you released during a treatment will return around you. I can assure you, it's not pleasant. Just remember that all you need to do is ask for them to be closed. I highlight this because I've experienced it myself and ended up with hundreds of wandering souls in my house! I had no idea what to do anymore!

The impact had to be strong enough for me to fully understand the rules. I had to grasp the law of cause and effect regarding wells of light in order to develop my ability to teach properly.

Some might find this unfair, but these tools are incredibly precious. We must not take for granted that beings of light will do the work for us. We each have our roles, and we cannot do theirs any more than they can do ours. It's actually extraordinary!

The goal is not to memorize everything by heart but to use your logic and your explanatory sheet if needed. It is truly a wonder to perform energy treatments consciously with all these vibrations of love that arrive to bring about modification, change, repair, or even perfect healing.

Messenger of the Source

Information is also transmitted to me when I accompany someone with many abilities. All I have to do is share what I receive. Like with the young Atlanteans, my client validates on their end the accuracy of the information I received for them.

Over time, I've accompanied many people, and every time, everything was accurate. Don't think it's easy. Well yes, it is easy— and at the same time, gaining complete confidence in your ability to transmit it can take quite a while.

At first, when I received these channelings, I asked my guides, my soul, and other light beings many questions. I would often say to them, "I truly want everything to be accurate, because if it isn't, it won't go well when I return to the Source!" I repeated that sentence so many times. Does this speak to you: the law of return? I told you that everything you say, do, or think will come back to you eventually. I can confirm that the guides never misled me, but you cannot imagine how many times humans have. I can't even blame them because it was me who fed the fear of passing along inaccurate information.

I believe that if you had to pass along these messages, you would also have doubted the truth of what I received through channeling. What greatly helped me in this process of trust was that very often, my clients had already received the same message, either in a dream or during meditation, but had not understood its meaning.

It's not always easy for me to live a normal daily life with those around me without feeling the urge to explain why they are going through certain experiences. Generally, people expect me to sympathize, but it's not possible for me to act that way. I prefer that they become aware of the origin of their issue.

Energetic Links

I asked my guides so many questions, but not really about myself. I moved forward in my exploration by discovering the makeup of the human being. One day, while performing an energy treatment on a client, I started to see energetic links appear. They were represented by a cord of light connecting my client directly to another person. I could see energy flowing from one to the other. It was not pleasant to witness it, as one was feeding off the energy of the other. I then learned how to release these energetic links.

On another occasion, one of my clients had her vision open, and when I began releasing this energetic link, another appeared, followed by several more. I believe I spent nearly four hours on this release, and each time she would tell me, "There's still another one!"

Honestly, I had to step out of the room. I burst into laughter and couldn't stop. It was just absurd, and thanks to that experience, I understood the importance of working with joy. That state increases the vibrational frequency, and information arrives faster and is more precise.

A link may represent one person or a large number of people. It may come from someone living or deceased who was part of our lives. These links may also connect to past lives. When I started asking questions to understand to whom the link belonged, I quickly realized that these answers often brought more discomfort than inner peace.

I had to constantly adapt, ensuring that it was clear to the person to know where the link came from. Of course, if I received a specific message, I allowed myself to pass on the information in its entirety. We are messengers and must offer all the messages we receive without questioning whether it's right or wrong to do so. We are not there to judge the content but simply to communicate it.

Sometimes people tell me, "I don't want to receive any messages." In that specific case, I won't receive any.

If you wish to explore this new concept, go immediately to page 151, Exercise #16.

Enjoy the discovery! Release of Energetic Cords

The Breath Through Conscious Breathing

Nowadays, more and more breathing practices are being taught. The more time you take to breathe out of love for yourself, the more your body will thank you. It's not easy to discuss the sacred in all things, as religion has greatly distorted the original meaning of what this pure and luminous aspect represented. Once again, it's up to you to ask yourself the following question: "Is it possible to breathe life? What must I do to achieve that?" Remember, it's simply a matter of asking or affirming—choose what feels best for you.

If you wish to experience this new concept, go immediately to page 153, exercise #17.

Enjoy the discovery! Breathe In and Out Within Your Physical Body

Now that you are more relaxed after completing Exercise #17, it's important to understand that everything starts from your heart. Every frequency you learn to vibrate within you will find its source in the heart of your heart. What's more, it will always be straightforward and incredibly effective.

Too often, humans feel alone in their existence. Many of them were not supported, cherished, or encouraged by their parents. That is no reason to deny oneself the right to embrace self-love and recognize that no one is ever truly alone. You have your personal guides, your guides of evolution and fulfillment, who are simply waiting to accompany you. Let's proceed with a small exercise to help you feel their presence.

Take the time to breathe as I've taught you. Once you feel well settled, address your personal guides and ask them to help you feel their presence, support, and companionship. Continue to breathe deeply and pay attention to your back. It is possible that it may straighten. It's also possible that you may feel as though you're wrapped in a cocoon of cotton. This is one of the ways your guides may reveal their presence to you.

Remember that everything should be simple and easy. For those who feel nothing or perceive no change, here are the questions to ask yourself: "Do I trust myself?", "Do I allow myself to receive what is most beautiful?", "Do I feel that I am worthy of receiving and feeling?"

Trust and faith are very important in the journey of discovering your creative power. Earlier, I mentioned that everything originates from the center of your heart, so don't wait any longer—move on to the next experience.

If you wish to experience this new concept, go immediately to page 157, exercise #18.

Enjoy the discovery! Rediscovering Confidence and Faith in Yourself

Chapter 4: Initiatory Journey and Training

During a training session in the Var region of France, I found myself in a place built on the ruins of a castle. To reach the small lounge, you had to go down a few steps. On one of them was a pot with a plant that seemed dead. Someone told me that the plant desperately needed help. I simply asked for the activation of the silver clover (this is the ideal energetic tool to provide a plant with everything it needs to be healthy) in the pot, and the plant moved. I've always loved these little manifestations, as long as no one was next to the plant and there was no draft either. I had ample proof that the tools of Atlantis were both very powerful and precise.

I had several conversations with the Specialists of Atlantis while I was there. When I received their teachings, their presence felt real, as if the scene were taking place in my living room. It was natural for me to understand, explain and know the specific sacred tools I had to use to bring the necessary vibrational changes to the physical body so that it could regain its natural healing power.

Throughout the years, I've had the joy of meeting various people during my numerous work trips and the initiatory journeys I organized in Egypt, Morocco, Tunisia, and Jordan. During these excursions, I always shared the various pieces of information I was receiving in the present moment, and I witnessed so many transformations. I greatly appreciated these exchanges and interactions. I conveyed the teachings about the place in real time. The knowledge conveyed in books and the one I was receiving were quite different.

During a trip to Jordan, we had to wake up at 4 a.m., because we had a bus to catch around 6 a.m. I headed to the shower, and the water was freezing! At that moment, I heard a woman say, "Where is Isabelle?" I didn't feel like answering since I needed all my courage to step into that cold water. A woman in the group was immersed in a past life. Based on what she was experiencing, she was about to give birth.

What was rather strange was that the woman she shared a room with had been born on that very day. Since we didn't have much time, as soon as the bus arrived, I asked one of the men in the team to take her into the bus. I needed to call on my guides to bring her back, here and now. I knew exactly what to do, even though it was the first time that had ever happened to me. I can tell you that I was relieved when the event ended.

I experienced many beautiful, mystical events throughout my travels. Everywhere I went, I used my energetic tools to cleanse places and harmonize hotels. I taught people how to raise the vibrational frequency of their food and neutralize the side effects of everything they drank or ate. In all these places, thousands of people had passed before us, leaving behind all kinds of disqualified energies. For everyone's well-being, it was easier for me to teach how to harmonize than to have to manage sick people. I took good care of each person who wished to receive my support. If I had to do it again, I wouldn't hesitate for a second. It was both magical and enchanting.

On another occasion, I was scheduled to attend a conference I was hosting. I had completely forgotten to energetically cleanse the venue beforehand. It turned out to be the worst conference of my life. I later learned that the room had been used for gatherings after funerals. There were so many wandering souls in that place, it was truly overwhelming.

Once in my car, I turned to the person accompanying me and asked her for a little help. My car was filled with those wandering souls. They were pulling on my crown chakra, and I felt my head spinning in every direction. Fortunately, my friend knew how to help me, and I admit she was of great assistance in that specific situation. I'm sharing this story so you can realize that before going to a place, you have the possibility to cleanse it before leaving home. In energy, everything that is asked happens instantly. There is no waiting time—"here and now" is the watchword. Following this cleansing, the people you will meet will be more pleasant and joyful.

Please note that this is not a harmonization of a living space but an energetic cleansing.

These are two different concepts.

If you wish to experience this new notion, go immediately to page 158, exercise #19.

Enjoy your discovery! Remote Cleaning of a Place

Now that you know how to cleanse a place before going there, you'll enjoy your shopping and visiting your parents and friends much more.

I suggest you run your own tests. Visit someone's place or a location without performing the cleansing, and the next time, perform the cleansing procedure. You'll see how different your visits will be. It's truly wonderful to take care of others and their living spaces. At the same time, taking care of yourself and your own living space is essential.

You won't have enough time to experiment with everything in a single day, but you can do a little bit each day. It's not necessary to be in a very quiet place where no one is making noise to perform these exercises.

The more you learn to act in the present moment and ignore everything happening around you, the more skilled you'll become at this.

During a trip to Egypt, a physical memory activated in my arm, and it felt as though it were being torn off. It really hurt. I was surprised that this happened at that moment. I needed to understand what was happening in the energy since, physically, my arm was still intact. It was a robotic memory. Through a past incarnation of my soul, during an intergalactic war, the person (if I can call it that) who had a robot-like appearance lost their arm during a violent impact. Doesn't that sound like pure science fiction? That's what I thought too, but it really hurt, and as soon as I accepted, acknowledged and released that physical memory, the pain completely disappeared.

I don't know if you've noticed, but the physical body is my greatest passion. As soon as I discover something new, I feel compelled to share it with someone. When I receive a new energetic tool, it's guaranteed that I'll need it for a session that same day, often within the hour.

During the training called "The Cosmic Specialists," which I taught in France over 10 years ago, a woman experienced a spontaneous healing during a group session. For about ten years, she had to use liquid eyedrops for her eyes because they dried out quickly. She had also worn glasses since childhood.

When she opened her eyes at the end of the session, her vision had improved and she even left without wearing her glasses.

What happened during the guided meditation was incomprehensible to her, but she chose to understand and agreed to speak to her eyes with sincerity. All this to tell you that the physical body sends you messages and is constantly waiting for you to acknowledge them by letting it know you've received them.

PART THREE:
POWERFUL INTEGRATION EXERCISES

The Basic Procedure

Before beginning an exercise, I invite you to prepare yourself by affirming the following:

♥ "I invite the archangelic plane to come and raise the vibratory rate so that it rises to the vibratory frequency of the Source of the Initial Sacred, of the Sacred Breast Initial, and to the sound frequency of the Sacred and the Sacred Breast Initial for me and for my place of living."

♥ "I ask for the opening of a well of light above me and my place of living." I invite you to ask if there are any protections around you; if so, ask whether you are authorized to release them. If yes, let the pure crystal fall of Atlantis pour down and check that everything has been released or dissolved. When that's done, say: "I connect heart to heart by a rainbow bridge to the power of the Force of Love." This represents: the love of God, of the Earth, of your Being of Light, of Divine Magic, and of the Order of Love.

♥ Say: "I learn to receive in order to give better. Through the same rainbow bridge, I connect to the light-heart of my soul, the light-heart of Gaia, the light-heart of all my guides, the light-heart of each part, aspect, multidimensionality and personality, and I circulate this power of love from one to another."

♥ Say: "I allow myself to descend and I place my feet on the light-heart of Gaia and I ask each part, aspect, multidimensionality and personality to place their feet with me on the light-heart of Gaia."

♥ Say: "I ask Gaia to let her sap of love rise to nourish my roots of light. I anchor myself deeply and I let Gaia's sap of love rise through my entire holistic Being. I allow myself to be cradled…"

As soon as you have finished the basic preparation, proceed with the exercise of your choice or conclude the procedure as follows:

♥ Say: "I thank myself as well as all the Beings of Light who accompany me for everything that has been done. I ask to bring the vibratory rate back down in a way that is right and perfect for me and my place of living. I also ask for the release of all rainbow bridges and for the wells of light to be closed now."

2

Release of the Impact of My Words and Thoughts

To begin, I invite you to do Exercise #1. Now place your attention on your heart. Then, take a few deep breaths and say:

♥ "I accept and acknowledge that I have often said: *name the destructive words as well as the thoughts.*"

♥ "I ask to release the destructive impact that these words have had on my respiratory and lymphatic systems and on my entire holistic body."

When you have finished, say:

♥ "I thank myself as well as all the Beings of Light who accompany me for everything that has been done. I ask to bring the vibratory rate back down in a way that is right and perfect for me and my place of living. I also ask for the release of all rainbow bridges and for the wells of light to be closed, now."

Freeing Oneself from Limiting Beliefs

To begin, I invite you to do Exercise #1. Now place your attention on your heart. Then, take a few deep breaths and say:

♥ "I invite my parents and all the people who passed their limiting beliefs onto me to present themselves before me in the energy."

♥ Say to them: "I thank you for all these beliefs you passed on to me. From now on, I return all your limiting beliefs to the light and I will learn to validate through my heart what truly aligns with me."

You may name these beliefs, such as:

Money is dirty... You have to work hard to succeed... You need to save for old age... You need a degree to be someone... The most important thing is to have a roof over your head... You must not lie or you'll go to hell... If you don't sleep for 8 hours, you'll wake up tired..., etc.

♥ Breathe deeply and let these energies go into the light.

♥ Say: "I thank them and ask these people to return to their respective dimensions."

And ask to close the wells of light, now.

Learning to Speak to Your Physical Body

I have put together some exercises for you to learn how to speak to your physical body. Always start by addressing the suffering part and say: "I am fully aware of…" and finish by saying: "I accept it and I acknowledge it." Here are several concrete examples to help you better integrate this concept. Before doing these exercises, it is important to accept seeing and accepting everything.

To begin, I invite you to do Exercise #1. Now place your attention on your heart. Then take a few deep breaths and:

For the eyes, say:

♥ "I accept and acknowledge that I have repressed many images that I no longer wanted to see in the different parts of my eyes."

♥ "I ask to release all these images and I ask that the special oil be poured to free the veils, the pressure and the tensions that these images have created in the different parts of my eyes…" Breathe deeply!

When you are done, say:

♥ "I thank myself as well as all the Beings of Light who accompany me for everything that has been done. I ask to bring the vibrational frequency back down in a right and perfect way for me and my living space. I also ask for the release of all the rainbow bridges and to have the wells of light closed, now."

For the ears, say:

♥ "I accept and acknowledge that there are many words I did not want to hear, as they hurt me, belittled me, degraded me."

♥ "I accept and acknowledge that I interpreted many words I thought I heard."

♥ "I ask to release all these words and all the sounds I buried in the internal and external parts of my ears."

When you are done, say:

♥ "I thank myself as well as all the Beings of Light who accompany me for everything that has been done. I ask to bring the vibrational frequency back down in a right and perfect way for me and my living space. I also ask for the release of all the rainbow bridges and for the wells of light to be closed, now."

For the feet, say:

♥ "I am fully aware that I haven't always wanted to live my life in my physical body, that I'm also not sure I want to do so. I haven't yet fully taken responsibility for my life. I sometimes feel I don't have my place on Earth or in my own life and I haven't always been aware of it."

♥ "I accept it and I acknowledge it! My feet, as I have received your messages well, I ask you to release the pain."

When you are done, say:

♥ "I thank myself as well as all the Beings of Light who accompany me for everything that has been done. I ask to bring the vibrational frequency back down in a right and perfect way for me and my living space. I also ask for the release of all the rainbow bridges and to have the wells of light closed, now."

For the ankles, say:

♥ "I am fully aware that I don't know what decision to make, that I am at a crossroads, that I also don't know what I really want to do. Rather than making the wrong choice, I prefer not to choose. I don't often make choices out of love for myself."

♥ "I accept it and I acknowledge it! My ankles, as I have received your messages well, I ask you to release the pain."

When you are done, say:

♥ "I thank myself as well as all the Beings of Light who accompany me for everything that has been done. I ask to bring the vibrational frequency back down in a right and perfect way for me and my living space. I also ask for the release of all the rainbow bridges and to have the wells of light closed, now."

For the knees, say:

♥ "I am fully aware that I have trouble accepting authority, that I sometimes experience confinement and feel imprisoned in my own body and life. Everything that is unjust easily triggers reactions in me like aggressiveness."

♥ "I accept it and I acknowledge it! My knees, as I have received your messages well, I ask you to release the pain and I thank you."

When you are done, say:

♥ "I thank myself as well as all the Beings of Light who accompany me for everything that has been done. I ask to bring the vibrational frequency back down in a right and perfect way for me and my living space. I also ask for the release of all the rainbow bridges and to have the wells of light closed, now."

For the pelvis, say:

♥ "I am fully aware that I do not feel very solid in my body, that my life does not quite represent what I wanted to accomplish and achieve. My life is going in all directions and it makes me feel insecure. Situations that weaken me also bring fragility to my pelvis."

♥ "I accept it and acknowledge it! My pelvis, as I have received your messages well, I ask you to release the pain."

When you are done, say:

♥ "I thank myself as well as all the Beings of Light who accompany me for everything that has been done. I ask to bring the vibrational frequency back down in a right and perfect way for me and my living space. I also ask for the release of all the rainbow bridges and to have the wells of light closed, now."

For the shoulders, say:

♥ "I am fully aware that I have often associated a burden to carry with my responsibilities and those I've taken on for others. Furthermore, I carry these people on my back and shoulders. It is time for me to return them to their own physical bodies and their own kingdoms."

♥ "I accept it and acknowledge it! My shoulders, as I have received your messages, I ask you to release the pain and all the weight."

When you are finished, say:

♥ "I thank myself as well as all the Beings of Light who accompany me for everything that has been done. I ask to lower the vibrational frequency in a right and perfect way for me and my living space. I also ask for the release of all the rainbow bridges and to have the wells of light closed, now."

For the elbows, say:

♥ "I am fully aware that there are conflicts in my family, whether between me and others or just among others. It affects me, and I wish everything could be resolved. Sometimes, I don't want to resolve things at all due to fear, apprehension and lack of courage."

♥ "I accept it and acknowledge it! My elbow, as I have received your messages, I ask you to release the pain."

When you are finished, say:

♥ "I thank myself as well as all the Beings of Light who accompany me for everything that has been done. I ask to lower the vibrational frequency in a right and perfect way for me and my living space. I also ask for the release of all the rainbow bridges and to have the wells of light closed, now."

For the wrists, say:

♥ "I am fully aware that I am not balanced between giving and receiving. I give too much and do not receive enough. My left hand closes every time I say 'no thank you' to someone who wants to give me something. My right hand closes when I've already given too much."

♥ "I accept it and acknowledge it! My wrists, as I have received your messages, I ask you to release the pain. I ask my physical and light hands to open widely and to regain dexterity and flexibility."

When you are finished, say:

♥ "I thank myself as well as all the Beings of Light who accompany me for everything that has been done. I ask to lower the vibrational frequency in a right and perfect way for me and my living space. I also ask for the release of all the rainbow bridges and to have the wells of light closed, now."

For the arms, say:

♥ "I am fully aware that I lack nurturing, that I did not receive the support and embrace of a parent, and that I do not know how to accept receiving from others."

♥ "I accept it and acknowledge it! My arms, as I have received your messages, I ask you to release the pain."

When you are finished, say:

♥ "I thank myself as well as all the Beings of Light who accompany me for everything that has been done. I ask to lower the vibrational frequency in a right and perfect way for me and my living space. I also ask for the release of all the rainbow bridges and to have the wells of light closed, now."

Learning to Speak to Your Human

To begin, I invite you to do Exercise #1. Now place your attention at the level of your heart. Then, take a few deep breaths and:

♥ Speak to the human within by looking yourself in the eyes in a mirror and telling them that its important that they listen to you and hear you.

♥ Tell them that everything you are doing is for them.

♥ Tell them that you truly need them to reclaim their place within you.

♥ Tell them that it is truly important that they accept to live on Earth and in your physical body at all times.

♥ Tell them that it is truly important to anchor themselves to the Earth and to let Gaia's Love nourish their heart, body, and mind.

♥ When you feel they are ready, ask them to jump into your body by placing their feet in your feet, their hands in your hands, and their eyes in your eyes to look straight ahead clearly.

♥ Once this is done, take the time to thank your human for choosing to trust you once again.

When you have finished, say:

♥ "I thank myself as well as all the Beings of Light who accompany me for everything that has been done. I ask to lower the vibrational frequency in a right and perfect way for me and my living space. I also ask for the release of all the rainbow bridges and to have the wells of light closed, now."

6

The Magnets of Your Humanity

To begin, I invite you to do Exercise #1. Now place your attention at the level of your heart. Then, take a few deep breaths and say:

♥ "I ask to receive and activate the magnets of my humanity in my hands." This will bring back the parts and aspects of you that flee to other vibrational planes and dimensions.

♥ Say: "I address each and every one of you. I understand that it's not easy to live in my physical body, that I feel pain, anguish, and sometimes anxiety. However, it is truly important that you return to your place within me, because it is for you that I am doing all this work of returning to love for myself and to what I came to accomplish on Earth."

♥ Open your arms and allow them to settle within you—you will feel more whole, more grounded as well.

♥ Thank them and ask them to no longer flee your physical body and your life.

When you have finished, say:

♥ "I thank myself as well as all the Beings of Light who accompany me for everything that has been done. I ask to lower the vibrational frequency in a right and perfect way for me and my living space. I also ask for the release of all the rainbow bridges and to have the wells of light closed, now."

Note: You will likely need to repeat this exercise often if you have long had the habit of fleeing your life and your physical body.

Radiating Gratitude in Your Life

To begin, I invite you to complete Exercise #1. Now place your attention at the level of your heart. Then, take a few deep breaths and:

♥ Ask your heart to activate its Sacred Radiance of Gratitude, and as soon as you feel this beautiful energy...

♥ Ask for it to intensify within you and for everything you have done, accomplished, and received throughout your life.

♥ Breathe deeply and let this beautiful energy vibrate strongly within you and all around you.

When you have finished, say:

♥ "I thank myself as well as all the Beings of Light who accompany me for everything that has been done. I ask to lower the vibrational frequency in a right and perfect way for me and my living space. I also ask for the release of all the rainbow bridges and to have the wells of light closed, now."

The Fountains of Light

♥ When you take your shower, visualize the stream as a fountain of light descending upon you.

♥ Think of something that brings you joy and focus your attention on your heart. Ask your heart to radiate love for yourself as you breathe deeply.

♥ As soon as you feel a vibration, an expansion in your chest, or simply a sense of well-being settling inside you...

♥ Ask for it to intensify, and you will experience this moment of Love for yourself. The more you practice this experience, the easier it will become to feel love.

This exercise is very powerful. You will realize that it's very easy to love others, but when it comes to loving yourself, it becomes much more challenging. And yet, this is the purpose of our return to Earth.

Liberation from the Dominant and Controlling Mind

To begin, I invite you to do exercise #1. Now place your attention on your heart. Then take a few deep breaths and think of something that brings you joy. As soon as you are ready, close your eyes and say the following:

♥ "I ask to be returned to emotional zero point." Wait a few seconds and continue your exercise.

♥ Ask for the activation of the sphere of neutralization of personal and collective thoughtforms (egregores).

♥ Ask that it activate in your unconscious, your conscious, your superconscious, and in your dominant and controlling mind. When it becomes light in the head...

♥ Ask to pour down the 8 balms, the angelic powder, and the interlayer balm.

When you have finished, say:

♥ "I thank myself as well as all the Beings of Light who accompany me for all that has been done. I ask for the vibrational frequency to be brought back down in a just and perfect way for me and my living space. I also ask for the release of all rainbow bridges and for the light wells to be closed, now."

Being in absolute neutrality, returning to zero point

Before carrying out an exercise or questioning your soul, make sure you are at zero point on the emotional level.

To begin, I invite you to do exercise #1. Now place your attention at the level of your heart. Then, take a few deep breaths, close your eyes, and:

♥ Think of something that brings you joy. As soon as you are ready… Say this: "I ask to be returned to zero point emotionally and psychologically."

Wait a few seconds and continue with your exercise or your questioning of your soul.

When you have finished, say:

♥ "I thank myself as well as all the Beings of Light who accompany me for all that has been done. I ask to bring the vibrational rate back down in a way that is just and perfect for me and my place of life. I also ask for the release of all rainbow bridges and to have the light wells closed, now."

Raising the Vibrational Frequency

♥ Say: "I invite the Archangelic Plane to come and raise the vibrational frequency of my entire holistic being and that it be elevated to the vibrational frequency of the Source of the creation of the Sacred Initial and the Sacred Breast Initial, to the sound frequency of the Sacred Initial and the Sacred Breast Initial for me and the place where I am. May this settle throughout me, around me, and may it stabilize."

Lower the vibrational frequency before going to sleep by saying:

♥ "I invite the Archangelic Plane to lower the vibrational frequency of my entire holistic being so that I may sleep a deep and restorative sleep."

Understanding and Honoring the Truth of Your Heart

To begin, I invite you to do exercise #1. Now place your attention on your heart. Then take a few deep breaths, and:

♥ Ask your heart to restore all communication circuits between your words, thoughts, and heart.

♥ Breathe deeply and pay attention to the energy flowing within you.

♥ Ask your heart if it hears you... Be attentive to the response.

♥ Ask your heart if you are honoring its truth... Be attentive to the response.

♥ Ask your heart to activate the Sacred Radiance of Forgiveness and to envelop all the lies you have told others and yourself.

♥ Be honest with yourself and others, and your heart will guide you in the best direction so that you may be happy and proud to be who you are.

When you are finished, say:

♥ "I thank myself as well as all the Beings of Light who accompany me for all that has been done. I ask to lower the vibrational frequency in a fair and perfect way for myself and my living space. I also ask for the release of all rainbow bridges and for the light wells to now be closed."

I suggest repeating this exercise whenever you realize you have been dishonest with yourself or others. Be kind and avoid judging yourself.

14

Releasing Memories of the Past

Take your notebook where you've written down the information that has not yet been released. Make yourself comfortable.

To begin, I invite you to do exercise #1. Now place your attention on your heart. Then take a few deep breaths, and:

♥ Think of something that brings you joy. As soon as you're ready, close your eyes and say the following:

♥ "I ask to be returned to emotional zero point." Wait a few seconds and say:

♥ "I accept and acknowledge that I still hold resentment toward *name the person and what you reproach them for*. It is time for me to free myself from it. That does not mean I agree with what they made me experience, but I accept and acknowledge that I have deeply lived it with my entire being."

♥ Breathe deeply.

♥ Ask to activate a personal and external emotional ejecting spiral, breathe deeply and let all the repressed emotional charge within you be released. As soon as this is done...

♥ Thank the person for having played that role in your life.

When you are finished, say:

♥ "I thank myself as well as all the Beings of Light who accompany me for all that has been done. I ask to lower the vibrational frequency in a fair and perfect way for myself and my living space. I also ask for the release of all rainbow bridges and for the light wells to now be closed."

Release of Emotional, Physical, and Psychological Empathy

♥ Ask for the opening of a well of light above you and the place where you are.

♥ Ask for the activation of an ejecting spiral of physical, emotional, psychic, and psychological empathy.

♥ Take time to breathe deeply.

When you feel that everything is light within you...

♥ Give thanks and ask for the well of light to be closed.

P.S. Be aware that several times a day, you may need to release the energies you feel from others.

Release of Energetic Cords

Here is a simple yet powerful exercise to cut energetic cords. You can ask if there are people attached to you through energetic links. If you wish, you may also ask to feel them. Be aware that everything is part of the law of cause and effect, so if people have created energetic cords with you, it means that you have created cords with others too. Remember that everything starts with the self. You can choose to panic or simply speak the following statements, which will bring you great liberation:

To begin, I invite you to do Exercise #1. Now place your attention at the level of your heart. Then, take a few deep breaths and say:

♥ "I accept and recognize that consciously or unconsciously, I have created energetic cords with others. I accept and recognize this."

♥ "I speak to all the people to whom I have been energetically attached: Thank you for the experience, but from now on, I release you from me and I release myself from you."

♥ "I invite Archangel Michael to come and cut the cords in both directions, and I ask for the activation of the sphere of gratitude to accompany these people back to their own dimension or to the heavenly realm (for deceased persons)."

When you have finished, say:

♥ "I thank myself as well as all the Beings of Light who accompany me for all that has been done. I ask for the vibrational frequency to be brought back down in a just and perfect way for me and my living space. I also ask for the release of all rainbow bridges and for the wells of light to be closed now."

This is the most fair and easiest method to free yourself from these energetic cords.

Breathe In and Out Within Your Physical Body

♥ Settle in comfortably. Take a few deep breaths while inhaling and exhaling within yourself. If any specific part of your physical body feels unwell, I invite you to direct your breath on the exhale toward the area that needs it. Remember that you are the master of your life and that your physical body responds to everything you say, do, or think.

♥ Next, do the same exercise when you take a bath or even a shower. You will quickly feel the benefits. The relaxation of your entire inner being will accelerate in contact with water, as it is synonymous with life. If you allow life to flow freely within you just by breathing, you will discover one of its immense benefits. Know that even today, everything experienced in water is multiplied. You have the opportunity to experience this as often as you wish. Isn't that magical? I am certain that by doing this simple exercise, you will feel the tension release and a space open within you. The more regularly you practice this exercise, the more you will feel your creative power in action.

18

Rediscovering Confidence and Faith in Yourself

To begin, I invite you to do Exercise #1. Now place your attention at the level of your heart. Then take a few deep breaths and say:

♥ Breathe deeply and when you feel calm settling within you, ask your heart to activate the radiance of confidence and faith for yourself. Do it using your voice, and when you feel either an expansion, a sense of softness, or any other manifestation, ask that it intensifies and grows. Channel this radiance into your digestive and respiratory system and say:

♥ "I accept and acknowledge that I have often doubted myself and my physical and psychic abilities. Today, I affirm that I have the right to feel confidence in myself, love for myself, and that I hold a special place in my own life!"

When you have finished, say:

♥ "I thank myself and all the Beings of Light who accompany me for all that has been done. I ask that the vibrational rate be brought back down in a right and perfect way for myself and my place of living. I also ask for the release of all rainbow bridges and for the light wells to be closed now."

This exercise will quickly allow you to experience great transformations in your level of confidence and faith in yourself, as well as help you reclaim the primary place in your life out of love for yourself. Isn't it simple and easy to do?

19

Remote Cleaning of a Place

How do you perform a cleaning of a place before going there? Learn to build trust and faith in yourself before beginning to practice space cleansing. When you feel ready, do the following:

To begin, I invite you to do Exercise #1. Place your attention at the level of your heart. Then take a few deep breaths and:

♥ Ask to activate powerful ejector spirals for personal and others' emotions to release all egregores of anger, fear, injustice, etc., present in that place;

♥ Ask to freeze the wandering souls so that they do not interact with you while you are there;

© Ask to pour all the power of the 22 Universal Laws into this place;

♥ Ask that the wandering souls be unfrozen after your departure from that place.

When you have finished, say:

♥ "I thank myself and all the Beings of Light who accompany me for all that has been done. I ask that the vibrational rate be brought back down in a right and perfect way for myself and my place of living. I also ask for the release of all rainbow bridges and for the light wells to be closed now."

Isn't it simple and easy? You just have to do it, and it will take as long as saying it.

You can connect to several places at once and cleanse them all at the same time.

158

Please note that cleaning a living space is different from harmonizing a living space.

Connecting to the Power of
Absolute Unconditional Love

To begin, I invite you to do Exercise #1. Place your attention at the level of your heart. Then take a few deep breaths and say:

♥ "I connect heart to heart through a rainbow bridge to the power of the Force of Love."

♥ Breathe deeply and let love come to you, and when you have truly felt it…

♥ Through that same rainbow bridge, connect to the light heart of your soul, the light heart of Gaia, the light heart of all your guides, the light heart of every part, aspect, multidimensionality and personality. Let this power of love circulate from one to the other.

♥ Learn to receive in order to give better.

When you have finished, say:

♥ "I thank myself and all the Beings of Light who accompany me for all that has been done. I ask to bring the vibrational rate back down in a right and perfect way for myself and my place of living. I also ask for the release of all rainbow bridges and to close the wells of light, now."

The most beautiful gift you can give yourself is to learn to love yourself truly. The more you allow your heart to vibrate with love for yourself and radiate its state of gratitude for life, the more you will recover the missing pieces of your life.

Note: It is important not to imagine things, but simply to let an image, a sensation, or even nothing at all come to you. What matters is learning to ask with the heart in order to receive.

Appendix 1

Life Lessons

A life lesson is experienced in this life as a return of approximately 2% of what was done in past lives.

Warning:

First and foremost, it is important never to say or think that you *were* this or that in past lives. Also, do not take on the emotional burden of these life lessons, since in no way did *you* have these experiences of a lack of love in your soul's past lives. You simply carry the memory of all that was experienced. This life is the first you are living as *who you are now*. It's very important to understand this. It will allow you to release these energies much more easily and without judgment toward yourself.

Know that this is surely the most beautiful thing you can do for yourself and to liberate your soul from all that past lived through lack of self-love. These life lessons made you go through many experiences that were not easy. It is time to be very proud and grateful toward yourself because, up to now, you have accomplished what you needed to in order to release these energies.

It took a great deal of determination and courage to return to Earth because your soul knew very well what you would have to go through, and it said "YES!" That means everything within you has been programmed for your success.

The impact of everything lived in the past incarnations of your soul that was never forgiven at the heart level will be experienced in this life — this is what is known as the Karmic burden.

Souls have chosen, before returning to Earth, to fully understand the consequences of these experiences so that they could place forgiveness in their hearts for all those less easy and luminous experiences.

They met with the Guide of Incarnation and carefully designed their life plan. These souls made this choice knowing full well that reliving all of it wouldn't be easy. And even though it sometimes seems impossible to get through without being completely shattered, they made a promise to themselves to succeed.

A group of souls even chose to represent the karmic burden of their soul family, their evolutionary collective, and their genealogy. This means that these souls would go through a multitude of experiences without ever knowing whether these life lessons belonged to their soul's incarnations or not. They knew they would need help, support, and guidance, but that it would only happen once the return to Self-Love was in place.

Life Lesson: Children

In this life, men and women who are sterile by birth or who have become sterile due to illness need to understand that in past lives, some incarnations mistreated, beat, poorly fed, confined, and even killed children. They thus made the choice not to have children in this life until this life lesson is forgiven, accepted, and consciously released.

Life Lesson: Murder

In this life, children who have very difficult relationships with their parents and who always feel in danger of death must understand that an incarnation of their parent ended the life of one of their soul's past incarnations. This information remained active in their cellular memory.

Life Lesson: Violence — verbal, emotional, physical, and psychological

In this life, people who have experienced any form of violence from a young age are often very gentle individuals with no inner violence. Most of them come to release the violence committed by their soul's past incarnations.

Life Lesson: Power, oppression, belittlement, manipulation, devaluation

In this life, people who went through these experiences often choose parents who are cold, distant, and unaffectionate. They will continue to encounter people similar to their parents. In past lives, their souls' incarnations used these energies to achieve their ends without any remorse.

Life Lesson: War

In this life, some people are drawn to professions involving weapons — police officers, special forces, military, GRC, CIA, etc. They carry within them a form of violence that needs to be released and channeled. Their souls' past incarnations participated in many wars, both terrestrial and intergalactic.

Life Lesson: Rape and Incest

In this life, men and women who suffered sexual assault (molestation, rape, or incest) are experiencing the effects of soul incarnations that committed rape or incest.

Life Lesson: Suicide

In this life, a person who experiences abandonment from a very young age, who frequently questions continuing life on Earth and who attempts suicide but does not die, is facing the life lesson of suicide. They are not allowed to end their life that way. Certain soul incarnations ended their own lives — and this is the deepest suffering a soul can carry.

Life Lesson: Belonging

In this life, a person who cannot live alone, who needs to belong to someone, a group, or a sect, who constantly seeks the approval of others and ends up being manipulated: this person's soul had incarnations that manipulated and controlled many others, making them believe they belonged to them and had to submit in silence.

Life Lesson: Verbal, emotional, physical, and psychological violence (repeated)

In this life, people who feel like slaves to their own lives, jobs, children, or society are often abused and manipulated, because some of their souls' past incarnations abused their own employees physically, morally, and emotionally.

Life Lesson: Religion

In this life, people who are demanding, severe and cold, and those who are alone, are often drawn to religious symbols — crosses, seals, or other religious objects. The reason is that their souls' past incarnations were married to God, belonged to religious orders (nuns, monks, priests), or were part of sects.

Life Lesson: Lying

In this life, some people frequently lie because they have never known what it means to speak the truth. For them, it will feel natural to tell lies, and in return, they will be lied to in many areas of their life. Some of their souls' past incarnations were masters of lying.

Life Lesson: Poverty, Theft, Embezzlement, and Fraud

In this life, someone who lives in poverty without being able to escape it, who sees no light at the end of the tunnel, who is easily scammed, who is diverted from their path or from a loved one, or who has their possessions stolen... will have had past soul incarnations that were very greedy, where they took others' possessions easily, and succeeded in diverting people from their paths, their loved ones, or their success.

Life Lesson: Genetic Manipulation, the Werewolf

In this life, some people give birth to a child affected by a rare or orphan disease, childhood cancer, polarity inversion (feeling male in a female body or vice versa, or organs reversed from left to right), with an undeveloped body part, or extreme mood swings. These people are often found in the fields of health, science, or research.

Some of their souls' incarnations performed many experiments in Atlantis. The results were disastrous, and people died as a result.

Life Lesson: Secrets

In this life, people who reveal almost nothing, who tend to keep everything inside, are often bearers of secrets. Some of their souls' past incarnations were part of secret orders or had taken an oath to reveal nothing. Others hid the birth of a child, or remained silent after witnessing a rape or incest, for example.

Life Lesson: Guides, Teachers, Therapists, Gurus

In this life, guides, teachers, therapists, and gurus who are manipulated, who suffer various energetic attacks on their third eye, solar plexus, or sacral center and who often have someone around them feeding off their energy... have had soul incarnations who have used their knowledge and skills for manipulative purposes. They connected to their clients' or patients' energy centers in order to better manipulate them and enhance their own extrasensory abilities.

Life Lesson: Magic and Sorcery from All Worlds and Universes

In this life, someone who is constantly affected by rituals, spells, or incantations, who cannot tolerate needles without fainting or having strong skin reactions, who easily manipulates the elements (like stopping the rain), who cannot follow a recipe without changing it and who seeks to relive a past incarnation as a shaman, had soul incarnations that heavily practiced a lot of black magic and used their gifts and knowledge for highly destructive and manipulative ends. Among their souls' past incarnations, we find magicians, shamans, sorcerers, alchemists, mages, druids, etc.

In addition to denial, there are the occult sciences, which are not well understood. Most people associate this science with magic or sorcery, but in reality, it is the science of *hiding* things. This means that even if an object is right in front of your eyes, you will not see it. You may have experienced sexual abuse in your childhood and have no memory of it. Hiding situations, events, objects, or people often leads to deep inner conflict. However, hiding does not mean erasing from memory, because as soon as this science is fully neutralized, the memories resurface.

Life Lesson: Control

In this life, people with strong mental control, those who need to verify everything before making a decision, who are rigid in their beliefs... have had soul incarnations that succeeded in controlling many people by manipulating them and making them believe anything in order to achieve their goals.

Life Lesson: Self-Sacrifice

In this life, people who can't put themselves first, who feel obligated to serve others, who neglect themselves to ensure those around them lack nothing... have had soul incarnations where they were served by others, that ensured people around them were always at their service, without rewarding or valuing them.

Life Lesson: Cannibalism

In this life, people who cannot swallow a piece of meat and are over 30 years old had soul incarnations that practiced cannibalism, not out of necessity, but as a conscious custom.

Life Lesson: Vampirism

In this life, a person whose vital energy is often drained, who almost always has someone energetically attached to their solar plexus, sacral center, heart, or third eye... had soul incarnations that consciously fed on the energy of others to feel important and appear better.

Life Lesson: The Animal, Mineral, Plant, Human, and Aquatic Kingdoms

In this life, people who are deeply committed to defending all causes related to the various kingdoms, who go so far as to protest, gather petitions, and even defend their points of view with violence... had soul incarnations that mistreated, abused, and destroyed the kingdoms through various means.

Life Lesson: Victimization

In this life, people who feel like victims of everything, who tend to always look for someone to blame (and it is never themselves) have had soul incarnations that mastered the art of blaming others in their place.

Life Lesson: Neglect, Suppression, and Belittlement

In this current life, individuals who have been neglected by their parents or family and devalued in the eyes of others have had past soul incarnations that did not care for the well-being of others and preferred to crush and belittle their own children or anyone who was different.

Life Lesson: Betrayal

In this present life, people who are betrayed by those they trust the most and often experienced pain in their shoulder blades, have had past soul incarnations where they were masters of betrayal and managed to convince others they were always completely innocent.

Life Lesson: Dependency

In this present life, people who become dependent on alcohol, tobacco, chocolate, chips, drugs — all those substances that often become their best friend — have had past soul incarnations who made others dependent on them, who took great pleasure in blackmailing them and forcing them to submit to their will.

Life Lesson: Devaluation

In this present life, people who were devalued by their parents from childhood, told they would never amount to anything, never succeed in life, or were not intelligent... have had past soul incarnations that devalued people who appeared more intelligent than they were. They made them believe they were a burden on society, that they should never have been born.

All these life lessons involve contracts, sub-contracts, pacts, and alliances. You will also find allegiances and objects linked with religion, cults, orders, slavery, purgatories, sacrifices, magic, witchcraft, voodoo, shamanism, and marabouts originating from Earth and the Multiverse.

One cannot improvise as a Master of karmic release — it requires a deep understanding of each life lesson, of the full constitution of the holistic Being, and above all, having completed one's own karmic liberation before assisting others in their journeys.

It is essential to be ready to accept and recognize that everything was chosen before incarnating, and that we are not victims but extraordinarily responsible beings. Nothing has been placed on your path that you are incapable of accepting and acknowledging in order to release the original source and free your soul from all these experiences of non-love for Self.

Thank you for saying YES to your freedom and the Power to Love Yourself!

Appendix 2

The 22 Universal Laws of the Multiverse

Here are the 22 Universal Laws of the great Multiverse. The first 7 Laws are those that govern Earth.

- **Joy**: Corresponds to the navel
- **Love**: Corresponds to the heart
- **Sharing**: Corresponds to the hands
- **Respect**: Corresponds to the nose
- **Truth**: Corresponds to the thymus
- **Justice**: Corresponds to the joints and nerves
- **Balance**: Corresponds to the pelvis, including the coccyx
- **Loyalty**: Corresponds to the digestive system
- **Pacification**: Corresponds to the knees
- **Righteousness**: Corresponds to the back
- **Rebirth**: Corresponds to the blood
- **Stability**: Corresponds to the feet and ankles
- **Emptiness**: Corresponds to the brain
- **Sensitivity**: Corresponds to the third eye
- **Fertility**: Corresponds to the reproductive system
- **Reliability**: Corresponds to hearing
- **Opulence**: Corresponds to the respiratory system
- **Ingenuity**: Corresponds to the eyes
- **Metamorphosis**: Corresponds to the glands
- **Honor**: Corresponds to the spleen and pancreas
- **Liberation**: Corresponds to the shoulder blades
- **Creatum**: Corresponds to the immune system

If you wish to experience the power of these radiances, here's how to proceed:

To begin, I invite you to do Exercise #1. Now place your attention at the level of your heart. Then, take a few deep breaths and say:

- "I ask my heart to activate its great Sacred Radiance of the Law of ..."
- Then direct it to the corresponding part of your body that needs it.
- Take time to breathe deeply and welcome the many benefits you will experience. You can continue with another law for as long as you feel it is right for you.

When you are finished, say:

- "I thank myself and all the Beings of Light who accompany me for everything that has been done.
- I also ask that the vibratory rate be lowered in a just and perfect way for me and my place of life.
- I also ask for the release of all the rainbow bridges and for the light wells to now be closed."
- Ideally, always ask out loud for what you want to receive. What you need to know is that these laws are very real. They were always in action until duality arrived on Earth. Children under thirty are very sensitive to the respect of these laws, and for some, it is truly not easy, because they feel an energy of injustice when they are not respected, and it hurts them deeply. The more you make these laws vibrate within and around you, the more you will consciously realize the power of these laws.

Appendix 3

Knowing When and What to Use Daily

In the Morning Before Getting Out of Bed

- Ask to realign the axis of your bodies of light with your physical body and say:
- "I jump into my body, I jump into my life."

In the Evening Before Going to Sleep

To begin, I invite you to do Exercise #1. Focus your attention on your heart. Then take a few deep breaths and say:

- "I ask for the opening of the time corridor of the day.
- I accept and acknowledge all the words, thoughts, and actions I have taken.
- I ask for the Sacred Radiance of the 22 Laws to be poured over everything present in this time corridor.
- I forgive myself for everything that was not for my highest good, and I express my gratitude."

When you have finished, say:

- "I thank myself and all the Beings of Light who accompany me for everything that has been done.
- I ask to lower the vibrational frequency in a just and perfect way for myself and my place of life.
- I also ask for the release of all rainbow bridges and for the light wells to now be closed."

Before Going to Work, the Grocery Store, Visiting Friends, etc.

- Do the space cleansing exercise.

After Each Consultation

To begin, I invite you to do Exercise #1. Focus your attention on your heart. Then take a few deep breaths and:

- Ask to activate an emotional ejection spiral, and a spiral to eject emotional, physical, and psychological empathy.
- Ask for the outpouring of the following balms:
- Turquoise, Scarlet, Violet, Orange, Silver, the Balm of the Past, of God and Diamond.

When you have finished, say:

- "I thank myself and all the Beings of Light who accompany me for everything that has been done.
- I ask to lower the vibrational frequency in a just and perfect way for myself and my place of life.
- I also ask for the release of all rainbow bridges and for the light wells to now be closed."

When the Mind is Going Too Fast

To begin, I invite you to do Exercise #1. Focus your attention on your heart. Then take a few deep breaths and:

- Place your right hand with fingers pointing upward at the center of your chest and breathe deeply.
- Then do the same with your left hand.

When you have finished, say:

- "I thank myself and all the Beings of Light who accompany me for everything that has been done.
- I ask to lower the vibrational frequency in a just and perfect way for myself and my place of life.
- I also ask for the release of all rainbow bridges and for the light wells to now be closed."

When You Feel a Sudden Sting in the Shoulder or Between the Shoulder Blades

To begin, I invite you to do Exercise #1. Focus your attention on your heart. Then take a few deep breaths and:

- Ask to activate the sphere of release of physical memories, breathe deeply, and when the pain has subsided, ask to return the sphere to the universal.
- Ask to pour out the following balms: regenerating, golden, rosy, and violet flame.

When you have finished, say:

- "I thank myself and all the Beings of Light who accompany me for everything that has been done.
- I ask to lower the vibrational frequency in a just and perfect way for myself and my place of life.
- I also ask for the release of all rainbow bridges and for the light wells to now be closed."

Conclusion

It goes without saying that not everything is as magical as you might wish. It requires perseverance to take one more step toward the truth of your heart. You have lived your life too often unconsciously with regard to the existence of the wonderful creative power that resides within you. It would have been extraordinary if these precious teachings you have just discovered had been taught to you in school.

The Earth is undergoing major transformation, and that does not mean these changes will occur easily, at least not until humanity realizes it holds within the powerful ability to create its life. It can manifest everything it wishes to see come to life in its everyday reality, for itself and for others, regardless of status.

Becoming aware that you are powerful creators is essential because the positive or negative impact of everything that comes out of your mouth or your thoughts makes all the difference in this world, where power and control are still very present.

The infinite potential of humanity is not tied to one's education or the job held in society, but truly to the consciousness carried in the soul's cellular memory. Whether you are 10 years old or 99, time only exists if you choose for it to exist. Know that it will always be possible to return to yourself as soon as you choose to. Many researchers on Earth work tirelessly to understand the functioning of the human brain. Yet by returning to oneself and allowing access to all that dormant memory linked to the knowledge of the Sacred Initial, the results would be much faster and more significant.

Are you one of those who have bought into the belief of fatality? It is time to do the exercise to free yourself from it, because I'll say it again—it's not what you learn in books from the past that will awaken within you such vast, pure, and powerful knowledge.

Being conscious at every moment is not easy to achieve. However, nothing is impossible for those who have faith and trust in their creative power. Learn and accept that the past is not the reflection of your future if you consciously choose for it not to be.

I have shared with you exercises that are both powerful and fair. You may or may not have tried them yet. Since you have purchased this book, when the time comes, you will experiment and find that nothing was left to chance.

Using energetic tools becomes a way of life as soon as you accept and acknowledge that you are made of 90% energy and only 10% physical matter. With this awareness, it becomes much more motivating and easier to give yourself permission to explore.

I invite you to ask yourself the following questions:

- What do you have to gain by being responsible for your own well-being?
- What do you have to gain by living with lightness of spirit?
- What do you have to gain by freeing yourself from the chains of the past?
- What do you have to gain by looking yourself straight in the eyes and saying: "From now on, I am the most important person in my life"?

I could write you hundreds of reasons to help you realize that everything becomes possible, that everything is within, and that everything transforms infinitely. But what would it bring you if you do not make the effort to return to yourself and write in your little notebook all that needs to be released, accepted, and forgiven?

Remember that it is my duty to teach you how to return to yourself, but I cannot do it for you. Remember the experience I had with my friend Gaëtan's pendulum—I definitely do not want that to happen again.

There are many tools, each designed to meet a specific need. Because the holistic body is quite complex, having access to this body of knowledge is very valuable. What makes these tools even more extraordinary is that anyone who can speak can use them and obtain great results.

Today, people who feel called to develop their senses, gifts and healing abilities can do so much more easily by using energetic tools. These tools are designed to restore the original, perfect form without any energy of power, or control. Remember, the body is composed of 90% energy and only 10% physical matter.

By visiting my website: https://isabellestgermain.com, you will discover my new ongoing program that teaches the functioning of the physical body, allowing you to perform complete energetic healings yourself.

The Atlanteans had truly foreseen everything. In those ancient times, they already knew what would happen on Earth thousands of years later. They used their knowledge to manifest all these tools so that when humans reached the soul state of self-love, they would have everything needed to rediscover their extrasensory abilities and spontaneous healing power.

I would love to tell you that no effort is required and that everything is magical—but what's harder to implement is quite simple: stop feeding any destructive energy toward yourself. Even if we deeply want to stop, it's so natural to continue. This requires multiple daily releases because everything regenerates quickly. But remember—it only takes time to ask, and the release happens just as quickly. It's just a matter of seconds.

If you've taken the time to complete the exercises I've offered, you must have already experienced wonderful results. It's important to cultivate a state of self-love to maximize your outcomes. No one but you will know whether you truly want to transform your life. Many people silently wish to leave this earthly life, without saying it aloud. But you cannot feed death and also want to live fully at the same time. You have to make a choice. You are the only one who can make that choice for yourself. So what will you choose?

All these beautiful energetic tools are waiting to be used by as many people as possible. They belong to no one in particular, and so they are freely accessible.

Will you be the next person to reclaim your birthright? Your right to what is most extraordinary?

If your answer is yes, I invite you to share your experiences with me. If you have any questions, don't hesitate to contact me at: **isabellestgermain2022@gmail.com.**

I have created a video program including 153 treatments to bring you knowledge of energetic tools and their proper use. This program is still available, and you can purchase it by contacting me. I will then send you all the details and the description of each treatment. I suggest completing these energy treatments, designed for holistic health, over a period of eleven months.

You will find a space on my website: https://isabellestgermain.com, where you can discover the 32 families of children currently incarnated on Earth from the great Multiverse. By exploring these universes, you will likely recognize yourself and identify the family your children belong to, thanks to the descriptions I have provided.

Do not let fate shape a life that does not reflect your dreams and desires. Take the time to experiment with the energetic tools to transform what limits you or holds you back from moving forward in your self-realization. I believe that each person on Earth today carries within them the knowledge of Atlantis. By reading the part related to it, you have the opportunity to connect, heart to heart, with all these extraordinary beings and to speak to them if you have questions. They will joyfully respond to you.

What's even more extraordinary is that over the years, I have opened many pathways so that humanity does not have to go through the same journey I had to undertake. This means it will be much easier for you than it was for me, as the door is already open and ready to be crossed.

I had made a promise to my Atlantean friends to pass on the knowledge of that island and its inhabitants. Now, I can say that I have honored my promise. I know that in the near future, I will write again to share the continuation of what this civilization wishes to transmit to us. For now, I know that I have written what needed to be shared.

Thank you for reading me and for daring to carry out the exercises I suggested. It touches me deeply.

I also thank this soul of mine for agreeing to return to Earth to bring forth all this knowledge. I dare to believe it will have made a difference in the lives of many human beings.

In Shared Humanity

With all due respect to humanity and our planet!

KOSHAM TAÏÉH! (I recognize myself in you!)

Isabelle St Germain

www.ingramcontent.com/pod-product-compliance
Lightning Source LLC
Chambersburg PA
CBHW051519120626
46551CB00012B/993